# ATTENTION AND ALIENATION

# ATTENTION AND ALIENATION

## THE INTERNATIONAL POLITICAL ECONOMY OF INFORMATION AND COMMUNICATION TECHNOLOGIES

### AARUSHI BHANDARI

Columbia University Press  *New York*

Columbia University Press
*Publishers Since 1893*
New York   Chichester, West Sussex
cup.columbia.edu

Library of Congress Cataloging-in-Publication Data
Names: Bhandari, Aarushi, author
Title: Attention and alienation : the international political economy of
information and communication technologies / Aarushi Bhandari.
Description: New York : Columbia University Press, [2025] | Includes
bibliographical references and index.
Identifiers: LCCN 2024059543 | ISBN 9780231208208 hardback |
ISBN 9780231208215 trade paperback | ISBN 9780231557313 ebook
Subjects: LCSH: Knowledge economy | Information
technology—Economic
aspects | Information technology—Social aspects
Classification: LCC HC79.I55 B49795 2025 | DDC 303.48/33—dc23/
eng/20250424
LC record available at https://lccn.loc.gov/2024059543

Cover design: Milenda Nan Ok Lee
Cover art: Roman Samborskyi / Shutterstock

GPSR Authorized Representative: Easy Access System Europe,
Mustamäe tee 50, 10621 Tallinn, Estonia, gpsr.requests@easproject.com

*To Neel, may the future be worthy of your light.*

# CONTENTS

*Acknowledgments*   ix

Introduction   1

1 The International Political Economy of Attention   13

Interlude 1: Baskin-Robbins in Kathmandu   43

2 ICT4D, Unequal Exchange, and Neoliberal Imperialism   46

3 Caste Society and Development Bait   73

Interlude 2: Being Extremely Online Against the Backdrop of an Armed Revolution   95

4 Social Movements, Counter Movements, and Discourse in the Attention Economy   113

5 Microdosing Collective Effervescence   144

Conclusion   182

*Notes*   *191*

*Index*   *211*

# ACKNOWLEDGMENTS

I t is an honor beyond words to acknowledge the many forms of personal and professional support and love that have made this book possible. I am overwhelmed that so many people have touched my life in these ways and enabled me to attain an impossible dream. My gratitude is ineffable; I will attach words to names in the hope that they convey a fragment of the intensity with which I feel these thanks.

Above and beyond all else, I thank my partner, husband, best friend, and soulmate—Kevin. The way you have made space in our lives for me to reach all of my potential is nothing short of a miracle. I never knew such a partnership could exist; one that is not only equal and equitable but reverent yet easy and effortless and always tremendously fun. Thank you for never balking at my "I'm writing" ire when you come to say hi. Thank you for making space for me to spontaneously blurt out writing ideas in the middle of a conversation about something entirely unrelated. Thank you for reading my drafts under made-up deadlines that I very strictly enforced. Thank you for giving me Neel. And thank you to Neel, for teaching me the wonders of play. At some point, writing this book felt like spontaneous play, and I would not be able to name this most extraordinary human experience without you as my teacher.

Speaking of teachers, Liz Cherry was my first sociology teacher when I moved to the United States for college, and I owe my entire career to her. She inspired me from the first day I sat in that classroom, and she continued to teach, support, and mentor me as the years passed. I am grateful to her for so much, including serving as the development editor for this book. She helped me take this book from a jumbled mess to what I hope is a coherent set of arguments that tell a coherent story about the internet. I am eternally grateful for her wisdom and support. I am also extremely grateful to Eric Schwartz, the acquisitions editor who saw my vision from the moment I sent him the first version of this book proposal. He gave me this incredible platform. Thank you for your endless support and enthusiasm for my work, Eric. None of this would be possible without you.

Thank you to my colleague Gayle Kaufman, who always encouraged me to pursue my ambitions and served as a real-world role model for what an exceptional leadership and mentorship truly looks like. Thanks you to my colleague Gerardo Marti, who has been incredibly supportive and always available when I needed to bounce my ideas off someone. Thank you to Kikie Seidi for your humor, strength and inspiration—our chats give me life, and I am so glad you are my colleague. Thanks also to Katy Fallon, my grad school advisor who has always been generous with her time and insights in both my academic and spiritual pursuits.

I must also thank my amazing students at Davidson College for always teaching me as much as I taught them. My gratitude is to my students generally, and specifically to students from the Spring 2024 Senior Seminar on Social Media, and the Independent Study on *Das Capital*, who pushed me to think about the theories and concepts in this book in new and creative ways. Thank you Nasir Jean Paul, Kamryn Walker, Allie Hay, Sophia Hanna,

Claire Wang, and Ben Kellogg. Talking through ideas about social media and Marx with you was among the peak experiences of my teaching life, and you helped me refine these ideas for this book. Thanks also to my students Victoria Anyanwu and Calli Robles for helping manage the various data collected for this book during summer research assistantships.

Thanks to my dear friends who have thought me worthy of their collaboration and helped build the intellectual foundations upon which this book stands. Thank you to Rebekah Burroway and Jess Kim being my collaborators and friends. Thank you to Sam Shirazi for doing both those things and also providing statistical consultations not only on this book but pretty much whenever I have a stats question; I am so glad I have a friend that loves stats as much as you do.

And thanks also to my friends who have enriched my life in so many other ways. I cannot find the right words to thank my best friend, Asmita Gauchan, who has been on the other end of my call almost every Wednesday for years as I worked through many parts of this book. It is a peak life experience to write together every week with the girl I met in high school who *somehow* was as online as me in the bizarre world of Kathmandu elites. You were the first person in my life to give me the strength to be myself, and it turned out that my true self was this nerdy internet person who wrote a whole book about it. Thanks to all of my other dear friends and family who love and accept me as this exact person and bring laughter to my heart and memes to my group chats. Thank you to my Davidson College junior faculty co-conspirators Meghna Chaudhuri, Sara Baugh, Vanessa Castaneda, Bassil El-zaatari, and Marcus Pyle: you all make me feel so grateful to be here. Thank you to my lifelong friends Joe Marchia, Bhinnata Piya, Dikshya Parajuli, Brandon McElrath, Krista Fjeld, and Alina Bejenari. Thank you to all my friends, too many to name individually, you have shined your light on my life.

I cannot finish this section without thanking *all* of my family. I have eight parents, and each of them brings a unique kindness to my life. Thank you to my incredible mom Reeta Bhandari and doting dad Prakash Bhandari. Thank you to my second parents Juni Tharu and Shyam Tharu, and my special little *bhai* Suhel Tharu. Thank you to my exceptionally wonderful in-laws Carol Wright, Jim McElrath, Thom Wright, and Myriam Mayshark.

Finally thank you to my late grandparents, especially the two that shaped both who I am today and how I poured myself into this book. Thank you to my *nani muwa* Laxmi Devi Pokharel, who was the epitome of strength, empathy, and kindness in the face of grave injustice. Thank you for opening the margins for me to break the cycles of ancestral trauma. Thank you also to *buwa* Dhundiraj Bhandari for believing in my potential from before I even remember, for telling everyone I was to become a *bidushi* when I was only five years old, and for showing me the path to an intellectual life of scholarship and supporting me in this world and beyond. I love the many, many conversations I have with you in my head, where I tell you how wrong you were to uphold the Brahmin status quo when you lived.

This book is the story of the internet, but it is equally the story of the granddaughter of these two exceptional human beings, standing at odds with one another in the annals of history. Thank you, dear reader, for going on this journey to the past and the future with me.

# ATTENTION AND ALIENATION

# INTRODUCTION

The history of the internet now spans more than three decades, which seems simultaneously too long and not nearly long enough for this technology to have become so central to the human experience. Information and communications technologies (ICTs) have certainly been central to *my* personal experience, and I want to share that aspect of self alongside the theories and data I provide throughout this book.

## A STORY TO EXPLICATE MY POSITION(S) IN WRITING ABOUT THE INTERNET

I was a twelve-year-old girl in Kathmandu, Nepal, when I got my first computer in 2002. Before my mother bought the computer, I was sailing along, daydreaming in gender-segregated classrooms with rote-memorization learning techniques that bored my imagination. I was silently and mentally protesting how everyone treated my brother better, how I couldn't go into the kitchen to grab a snack when I was on my period due to made-up Brahmin society rules, and how I wasn't allowed to use my voice when the world around me felt wrong or unjust, which happened often.

When the computer came, I was so grateful that my brother quickly lost interest in it after a few initial days of enthusiasm. So much in my world was his, but this amazing object slowly became *mine*. It's almost laughable how deeply I bonded with my first computer, but at that age it was truly the best thing that had ever happened to me: a nearly spiritual experience. Then followed the slow and staggering dial-up internet and suddenly, *magically*, I could find answers to so many of the inane questions that popped into my head throughout my life. All of a sudden, there was a mechanism through which I could engage my own distinct and elaborate imagination. I had never dared to entertain the possibility of *actually getting answers* before this point. In the few instances when I had asked questions in school or in other settings, I had been berated at best, beaten at worst. It occurs to me now that the adults around me didn't have the answers either, and my questions must have invoked some deep sense of insecurity that made them lash out.

People generally have the ability to get answers now, for better or for worse. Perhaps new kinds of problems are emerging because people are getting answers to questions they had never even asked.

But there was no denying the absolute magic in the new possibility of finding answers for me in 2002. For the first time in my life, I didn't feel so alone. As a confused kid with intellectual curiosities that defied my immediate surroundings, I now had the ability to go somewhere else. To folks looking at me at home, I remained physically present in my room playing with the newest gadget our family was showing off that we could buy. But in my experiential reality, I was everywhere but in my home: I was all over the world, talking to all kinds of people about all kinds of things! There was a whole world outside of my world inside my computer, and in this world I felt completely and hopelessly *alive!*

The escape I found online was particularly remarkable considering that outside my computer, outside my walls and the safety of my privileged Brahmin household, the Nepali Civil War was raging on the streets.[1] The guerilla warfare ended in 2006 with the success of the Maoist Party of Nepal overthrowing the monarchy and establishing a peoples' republic. During the early 2000s, the autocratic king Gyanendra Bir Bikram Shah instated one of the first authoritarian shutdowns of modern ICTs, such as mobile phones and the internet, in recorded history. The week without dial-up internet in 2005 was not only particularly bleak for my teenage self but also was a catalyst for King Gyanendra Bir Bikram Shah's downfall. People in Kathmandu did not take well to cutting off ICTs, even though it was so new we had barely accepted the magic of mobile telephony. I personally took it very poorly, concerned more at that time with my own inconvenience inside than with the revolution outside.

During these early and highly unusual years of my dial-up journey, I also came to terms with my own limitations, and that of my community and society. Everything I had been told was *real* until now was simply one way of doing reality, which was largely limited to the cultural practices of a tiny country sandwiched between the giants that are India and China. Reality had so many other iterations, there were so many other ways to live and be outside of my limited perception. As I "met" more people from more countries and places across the world, I was transfixed by the many ways different societies organized themselves and by the variety and mutability of what societies could and did look like across the world. Ironically, I never considered at the time that the revolution outside my walls was also interested in some kind of social reorganization.

One silly example of how the internet shaped my life is that I learned to write well in English because of my active engagement with the *Harry Potter* fan fiction community. There was nothing more joyful for my fourteen-year-old self than receiving comments from strangers from all over the world saying my writing made them feel things. It was an extraordinary experience, and I have pretty much never stopped writing since then. My writing evolved from fan fiction to college essays to graduate theses to research articles to this book. That journey directly led me here.

When I think about the journeys of the women in my family tree, I am so humbled by my own journey and so grateful to the role the internet has played in bringing me here. My own mother, and her mother before her, were victims of Brahmanical child marriage. My grandmother Laxmi Devi Pokharel's marriage was arranged in rural Nepal when she was eight years old. She was an extraordinary woman: she taught herself to read and write while herding sheep, and much later in life catalyzed herself as the only dominant-caste person in Bardia district to be revered by local Maoist insurgents. She could not have imagined my agentic life. It took a lot more than that first computer to get me here, including the sacrifices of my parents, changing sociocultural expectations for girl children among the urban elite, and many random elements that I cannot account for. But the computer was an integral part of the journey.

As the years passed, I clung to cyberoptimism, even cyberutopian visions for society as a whole. *If my own life could be so dramatically and radically altered by these technologies, how could they not alter the world at large?*

As readers of this book will note in the following chapters, a lot has changed about how I view and interpret this technology as a scholar and as an individual. A lot has changed, but I remain, at my core, an optimist. A utopian, even. Given my history, it's difficult to be any other way.

## THE STRUCTURE OF THIS BOOK

This book is a little bit about me, a little bit about the world, and quite a bit about the political economy of attention, and how it proliferates in the macro-, meso-, and micro dimensions of global society. In the three-plus decades during which information and communications technologies have become household necessities, what characteristics have these technologies adopted? In the foundational theory chapter, I describe the emergence of the attention economy as the first successful monetization strategy for the World Wide Web. Such monetization would not have been possible without the transition from Web 1.0 to the smartphone revolution and Web 2.0.

Throughout this book, I argue that ICTs via Web 2.0 economies of attention create conditions for *unequal exchange* between attention and alienation.[2] Users "pay attention" to receive mental health struggles that upon deeper investigation reveal an evolved form of Marxist alienation in which the bodies *and now minds, creative intellect, and emotions* of the online proletariat are exploited to generate capital for the ruling class.

This process of unequal exchange iterates on the *macrolevels* of ICTs and international development, the *mesolevel* of online social movements, and the *microlevel* of individual internet users. The key research question guiding this book is this: *How do ICTs foster unequal exchange between powerful and less powerful countries, social movements and counter movements, and ruling technological elites and the online population?*

At all three levels, the proletariat pays *in the form of both money and attention* to access the theoretical power of instantaneous information and communication. At each level, proletariats bequeath their very selfhood: personal data, knowledge about who they are at their most intimate core, and what they do and how they feel when the world is limited to themselves and the one device that contains the entirety of human possibilities. Selfhood now assumes exchange value outside of its original use value: to journey through the human experience, uncatalogued. Every aspect of the self is catalogued the moment one picks up a Web 2.0 device, and this information is then sold in a market where it can be used for purposes ranging from targeted merchandize sales to deep state espionage. The possibilities are limitless with the currency of attention.

Like traditional currency (money, in the Marxian conception), the economy of attention relies on the efforts of the proletariat for its growth and reproduction. Unlike traditional currency, however, *attention is naturally occurring, and limited and tethered to the bodies of humans directly.* Thus any exchange in which the proletariat pays attention for the profit motive of an external ruling class entity and receives none of the profit—i.e., nearly all online exchanges in Web 2.0—is inherently unequal. However, unequal exchange of attention does have theoretical advantages for the proletariat compared to unequal exchanges of wealth. In the Marxian conception, inequality in the material economy and the alienation thus produced is theoretically overcome by the violent overthrowing of the ruling class. This is deemed necessary because capital, existing outside of the natural order, must become, *can become* eliminated. Attention cannot become eliminated, only refocused.

The way to overcome alienation in this new economy is to reclaim power over one's selfhood individually and to work together to design new systems of ICTs (Web 3.0 and beyond) that maximize collective well-being. This is easier said than done because Web 2.0 platforms invest massive amounts of capital to implement algorithms designed explicitly to suppress power over our own attention. Yet, with the right focus and right intention, change is possible in this realm without inciting more violence than what is already perpetuated in capitalism. What kind of impact such change will have on the material economy and offline society is difficult to predict; however, a transformation of such magnitudes in the spaces where our collective minds are captured clearly has the potential to affect the spaces where the bodies inhabiting those minds are located.

In this book, I argue that an unequal exchange of attention and alienation iterate in cross-national political economy across international development, social movements, and individual use paradigms. I then argue that two kinds of shifts are critical to overcome this inequality: (1) healing and mental well-being at the individual, relational, and community levels, and (2) development of new web systems that not only focus on the technical architecture (e.g., decentralization, encryption) but also the *social quality* (e.g., eliminating comment sections, videoconferencing-based social learning spaces) of technologies that support reclaiming individual and collective attention for the purposes of individual and collective transformation.

## METHODOLOGIES

In constructing the arguments laid out throughout this book, I draw upon two ways of knowing that are, on the surface, antithetical. On the one hand, I use quantitative data and methods that align with Western enlightenment epistemologies, emphasizing empiricism and objectivity.[3] On the other hand, I honor postmodern, feminist, and Indigenous epistemologies that reject the possibility of objectivity, especially when describing social phenomena.[4] Sociology is among the few fields in which both epistemologies thrive, but usually they thrive in separate lanes.

My own inclination is that both ways of knowing are equally important in trying to decipher "truth(s)" about social reality. A complete analysis of any social phenomenon provides empirical data, and acknowledging the analysis of the empirical data never occurs in a vacuum.

In other words, *whatever I conclude about any data I share, I conclude because of how I am trained to view the world given my unique journeys, positions, experiences, biases, and worldviews.* Rather than proceeding to tell the story of the internet as though I am a neutral observer, in this book I chose the path of sharing my own story consistently and honestly to the best of my ability. This way the reader understands who is making these conclusions, and why I am motivated to interpret data and research as I do throughout this book. My own stories infused throughout these pages serve as autoethnographic accounts of an unusual life lived by a lover of the internet from the Global South.[5] Among other things, I hope they serve to convey that it is difficult for me to be so critical of a technology that has touched me so deeply; and ultimately, I hope the reader understands why my relentless, stubborn optimism sustains against a status quo that feels so bleak.

Having witnessed firsthand a national revolution and simultaneously the transition from Web 1.0 to Web 2.0, I innately believe that radical transformations *can and do occur* in both how societies and the internet are constructed. Belief, of course, is not empirical evidence, but it most certainly guides how I interpret evidence.

In chapter 1, I deal with theory only, building on the works of Karl Marx and the Marxist technology scholar Christian Fuchs to describe the shape of the world attention economic system.[6] The empirical evidence and quantitative data that support my cross-national arguments in chapters 2–4 are drawn from existing secondary sources, including the World Data Bank, the International Telecommunications Union (ITU), International Yearbook of Organizations (IYO), the GSM Association (GSMA), and the *Mass Mobilizations Data Project*.[7] In chapter 5, I move away from quantitative methods and fuse stories from my own life experiences with existing research to make my arguments.

I am deeply inspired by the recent works of Ruha Benjamin and Jenny Odell (among others) in treating my own experiences as valuable tools around which arguments about changing society are constructed. Benjamin does this expertly in her 2022 book *Viral Justice: How to Grow the World We Want*, and Odell juxtaposes art history data with her own stories in her 2020 book *How to Do Nothing: Resisting the Attention Economy*.[8] In some ways, this book is a spiritual successor to both works as it deals with issues of contemporary technology and the attention economy, anchored by stories of my own journey. Like Benjamin and Odell, I too end the book with proposed solutions for radical change and transformation. The similarities are only thematic because I use quantitative cross-national data and methods rather than qualitative cultural data and art. By adding these cross-national findings, I hope to ultimately make similar arguments about transformation and contribute to the current knowledge on ICTs, self, and society.

## CHAPTER SUMMARIES

Before delving into the data and narratives, chapter 1 serves as a foundational theoretical overview in which I describe the concepts of attention, alienation, and the international political economy of ICTs. I draw from Marxist and world-systems literatures that inform the theoretical conception of the world attention economic system and technologically unequal exchange. This chapter sets up the theoretical basis for the whole book.

The first interlude *establishes my social position as a child growing up in the high society of "development elites" of Kathmandu, Nepal.*

In chapter 2, I argue that attention and alienation is a specific form of *unequal exchange at the macrolevel* of international development. Reviewing the history of "development" as a concept, as well as organizations such as the UN that proliferated development, I argue that ICT for development (ICT4D) follows a neoliberal premise that harms Global South populations. Beyond the historical premise, the exchange between attention and alienation is uniquely harmful. Recent data from the GSMA for twenty-seven countries shows that, as Global South populations using mobile phones expand, most people use them to access social media sites that are deeply integrated into the attention marketplace.

Chapter 3 continues to draw out the argument that *unequal exchange* is a prominent historical pattern in international development, long before the advent of modern ICTs. Here I focus on the internal inequalities within Nepali society that facilitate uneven development. Development has historically served the national ruling class—in the case of Nepal, the dominant-caste cosmopolitan development elites, who shun the rural oppressed masses of subjugated castes, who they purportedly serve. Adding ICT4D to this paradigm allows these elites to further exploit rural populations as development bait. The way "development" was constructed from its conception has supported the ability of national elites to determine what the masses in Global South countries need. In the case of ICTs, the attention economy serves ruling classes, so ICT4D programs are compatible with the ruling agenda.

The second interlude *describes my experience growing up as an internet-obsessed teenager during the Nepali Civil War.*

Chapter 4 transitions to the *mesolevel* to focus on social movements. I discuss the history of online social movements and counter movements over thirty years, arguing that tensions between online social movement activity and outcomes that are manipulated by algorithms are designed by the ruling class to benefit from the attention economy. Using data from the *Mass Mobilizations Data Project*, I demonstrate how nation-states work with the tech ruling class to stifle online social movements. The data show how states handle violent protests through violent responses, whereas the technological ruling class handles nonviolent protests through algorithmic manipulations. I draw on the ASID model for socioeconomic development—agency, structure, institutions, and discourse—to demonstrate how discourse visible online is manipulated by multiple agents across different levels of power.[9] Unequal exchange in discourse occur when the technological ruling class uses increasingly sophisticated algorithms to exercise disproportionate power over virality. The algorithms manipulate users by compelling them to engage in discourse, and the users themselves are left drained from online interaction and engagement. In this way, the attention economy stifles social movements with clear and distinct "alternative imaginaries" that threaten the ruling class in the capitalist world-system. One way the stifling occurs is by manipulating and draining emotions so they engage in what some scholars describe as "slacktivism."

In chapter 5, I draw attention to the *microlevel* of individual online users. Anchored in stories from throughout my own life, I reiterate arguments from chapter 1 regarding how the current Web 2.0 attention economy cannot be a tool for transformation because it is already the tool of exploitation for the ruling classes. The unequal exchange of attention for alienation is highly profitable, especially in a time of waning material resources. There is no incentive for the ruling class to improve this. By emphasizing healing and the design of entirely new systems, the cycle of attention and alienation can be broken to achieve transformation and liberation. My key argument in this chapter is that healing is praxis. Web 3.0 and onward need to think beyond the technological systems (encryption, ownership, decentralization) and toward connected social systems (videoconferencing, community, collective well-being). I provide concrete examples of radical alternatives proposed by sociologists like Ruha Benjamin and Firuzeh Sookoh Valle.[10]

In the conclusion, I revisit my final arguments and describe my "ideal visions" for the future of the internet. I also revisit Erik Olin Wright's classical example of Wikipedia, an existing utopia that illustrates the internet at its best possible utility, and I describe what the internet still can be upon forgoing the attention economy in future iterations of the World Wide Web. The only limit is our imagination.

# 1

# THE INTERNATIONAL POLITICAL
# ECONOMY OF ATTENTION

To set up the theory of the international political economy of attention, in this chapter I outline the paradigms that inform the logic underpinning the chapters that follow. The theories underlying the arguments in this book draw primarily from Marxian and neo-Marxian perspectives on political economy. Specifically, I draw from Karl Marx's conception of capital, labor, and social reproduction in *Capital*, and his conception of alienation in the "Economic and Philosophic Manuscripts of 1844."[1] Neo-Marxist perspectives of world-systems analysis expand Marxist ideas to describe relations between nation-states rather than between labor and capital.[2] These theories are also central to the arguments laid out in this book, which I write from the United States—where I currently live and the hegemonic state apparatus of the ruling class concentrates—but with a direct focus on broader, cross-national implications.

The processes of unequal exchange between attention and alienation iterate globally, and this book follows a macro- to microstructure: the cross-national implications are explained in the early chapters, followed by the mesolevel social movement implications, and ending with the individual, microlevel implications. At each level, some form of unequal exchange occurs, wherein the online proletariat pays attention to receive alienation while the ruling class extracts their selfhood to generate a profit. However, this process takes on unique forms when it's nations versus other nations and global institutions, social movements versus counter movements, and online labor versus the technological ruling class.

At present, Marxist theories applied to the attention economy phenomena most notably appear across the robust scholarship of media and communications by the sociologist Christian Fuchs.[3] In explaining the concepts of attention and the attention economy, and setting up the theoretical basis for this book, I expand primarily on the works of Fuchs—especially by constructing the conceptions of a world attention economic system—along with the works of the digital arts scholar Jenny Odell. Although Odell does not draw from Marxist perspectives as Fuchs does, she has led the path in critical attention economy studies. Odell's book *How to Do Nothing: Resisting the Attention Economy* makes comprehensive arguments against the threat of the online economy.[4] I am also inspired by Odell's emphasis on place, positionality, and perspectives in interpreting the attention economy.

Bringing together these bodies of work—as well as additional research done by scholars on one or more of these topics—explain at the basest levels what I mean by "the international political economy of attention." Although the following chapters start with the global level of analysis and end with the individual level, in this chapter I reverse the explanations of relevant theoretical paradigms to enhance conceptual clarity. I begin with the most foundational concept of the attention economy, then capital, then labor, and then I describe how an evolved form of alienation socially reproduces the attention economy. Finally, I outline the theory of the world attention economic system to set up an explanation of technologically unequal exchange at the global level of analysis.

## THE ATTENTION ECONOMY

Before the U.S. Telecommunications Act of 1996, a world in which the internet functioned much like a public library or public parks was possible: free "third" spaces that are allowed to exist without socially reproducing the economic system of capitalism.[5] The technology was new, and many early adopters and creators of World Wide Web platforms had not actualized it as a profit-generating enterprise. In the early decades following the Washington Consensus, a key focus of nation-states—following the leadership and manipulation of the United States and United Kingdom governments—was to ensure that many aspects of society could become privatized.[6] During this period, neoliberalism became the status quo of economic systems around the world.

Neoliberalism is an extreme form of free-market capitalism that pushes privatization of social sectors, trade openness across markets and nations, and drastic reductions in government services and interventions. As neoliberalism became the status quo economic system and cultural ethos during the 1990s, public services and government assistance were demonized and minimized whenever and wherever possible. It is in this golden age of austerity that our favorite technology was born and popularized among lay users. Had the internet arrived at a different historical location, perhaps comments sections would not exist on social media sites. Unfortunately, information and communications technologies (ICTs)—dial-up internet, early broadband, and first generation *unintelligent* mobile phones—captured the collective imagination throughout the 1990s when Margaret Thatcher's "there is no alternative" messaging about neoliberal capitalism had become a self-fulfilling prophecy.[7] The Telecommunications Act of 1996 opened up the possibility for the World Wide Web to be monetized, privatized, and owned, planting the seeds for what we experience today as the attention economy.

The first iteration of the social internet, known as Web 1.0, began shortly after 1996, not having yet mastered the monetization of this technology.[8] During the "dot-com bubble burst" at the turn of the millennium, various companies that had the first chance to profit off this technology went out of business.[9] Other early profiteers such as Amazon narrowly escaped and later become the largest owners of the technological means of production—cloud storage. Today Amazon Web Services (AWS) serves as the landlord for the vast majority of data that is stored in physical server locations that are indivisible and seemingly magical to the lay users of the modern internet.[10]

Needless to say, the allure of the World Wide Web survived the dot-com crash of 2002. But the social media platforms—Myspace, forums, and message boards—that popped up early in the new millennium did not have a successful formula for monetization. There were ads, of course. But the generic ads did not capture the interest of most users who had to make a physical commitment to sitting down at their computers to engage this bizarre new form of social interaction. This was the nature of Web 1.0. You had to opt in to access websites of interest, and they tried to sell you things. Most users would not want to buy the things they were selling and would have enough tech-savvy not to click. Very much unlike this T-shirt I am currently wearing, which I ordered from the TikTok shop after it showed me an ad for wearable merchandize describing a fictional city from a fantasy novel I adore. I am writing this book, and even I am not immune. Targeted advertising through algorithms that intimately know me is *that effective*. Only my closest friends and loved ones and my algorithm know me well enough to serve me this particular T-shirt. Myspace could never.

Even with the green light from the 1996 policy, the attention economy as it exists today could not exist without a revolution in mobile telephony. In 2007, Apple released the iPhone and everything changed. The neoliberalization of World Wide Web technology finally paid off, and then some. The attention economy entered the chat. The invention of the iPhone ended the "opt in" era of web browsing. Using the internet was no longer an activity outside of one's everyday boundaries of the self. Instead the online world became a shadow of the self, following the body wherever it goes. Moreover, it became an *intelligent, multidimensional* shadow that could produce a sound that interrupted everyday activities and orchestrated a transition of focus away from the body and into the device—just like a ringing landline telephone. But a three-dimensional human being was no longer on the other end; instead we connected with an algorithm whose sole motive was to keep us tethered to the device so it could feed on our selfhood—like a parasite.

When a new wave of social media giants such as Facebook and Twitter (now X) developed mobile applications with increasingly sophisticated algorithms, the shadow-parasite became the most profitable outcome of the World Wide Web revolution. The currency it traded was our attention. Economies of attention existed in some capacity before this; in 1997, Goldhaber wrote the pioneer text "The Attention Economy and the Net," which was among the first to discuss the nature of attention as a scarce resource that may be converted to currency outside of material reality.[11] Through mobile telephone and increasingly sophisticated algorithms, Web 2.0 has taken the potentiality of information as currency and turned it into a thriving process of accumulation. Long before this time, in *Das Capital* Karl Marx characterized labor as an act of forced capture of attention: "apart from the exertion of the working organs, a purposeful will is required for the entire duration of [work]. This means close attention."[12] Web 2.0 and mobile social media has made capitalizing on attention—with or without "working organs" as physical ability is less relevant than a working internet connection—a truly indispensable wing of capital in the twenty-first century.

Simply defined, the online attention economy is a process of capital accumulation that relies on extracting the time, focus, mental fortitude, creative spirit, and emotional energy from the human body. Before the era of algorithmic shadow-parasites, creative spirit and emotional energy were difficult to profit from at this scale. Throughout modern history, examples like the weight-loss industry and the beauty industry illustrate marketing efforts that seek to capitalize on the insecurity primarily of women and feminine-identifying people.[13] These efforts relied, of course, on generic stereotypes on what a certain type of person may theoretically feel. The algorithm does not dwell in theories and stereotypes; the algorithm *mines information*. In other words, it *knows*. It knows because each user directly feeds the parasite every day through all mobile online activity.

Now everyone is uniquely vulnerable, and every emotion is uniquely profitable. The capital thus generated is not subsequently redistributed among the human bodies from where their qualities of being are extracted. Instead, the profit is retained among a small number of people who own Web 2.0 platforms who become the technological ruling class. Everyone else serves as what I describe as "the online proletariat."

## CAPITAL AND THE ATTENTION COMMODITY

Karl Marx notes several times across volume 1 of *Das Capital* that capitalism is a mode of production and exchange that evokes "material relations between people and social relations between things." Marx describes this process chiefly in the context of commodity exchange: when two owners of a certain commodity or property meet to conduct an exchange, they see each other not as fellows but as owners of desired property. Their interaction is material in nature: they determine the exchange values for each commodity based on their particular use values and engage at the level of ownership of material things. The things serve some social need such as sustenance or clothing or labor-power and compel the interaction between its purveyors.

Although Marx could not possibly have intended for such an extrapolation to be applicable centuries into his future, it is difficult to imagine the state of *social relations between things* more literally than smartphones that grant access to "social" media. Social media interactions, after all, are bits of data exchanged across physical things that gain social meaning via the interaction between things. Like the traditional market, social media is a space in which things—devices, algorithms—compel people to engage with each other. In addition, social media remains a market of exchange, but the product is people—users—who are generally under the impression that they are receiving a free "service." Web 2.0 platforms such as Facebook, X, and TikTok are "free to use" markets that depend on users choosing repeatedly to exercise their freedoms to return to this marketplace.

Some social media platforms take the "material relations between people" concept even more literally. Snapchat, for example, "rewards" pairs of people for maintaining communication "streaks" through engagement with the Snapchat platform, encouraging users to interact daily through this virtual "reward mechanism." The most fascinating element of the Snapchat system, however, is that when a streak is broken—when a pair fails to connect over Snapchat one day—they can reinstate their "streak" by making a monetary payment to Snap Inc. This gives the impression that connection has been maintained between two people who know very well that the connection is already broken. The connection is a means to the rewards end, yet the reward is nothing but a concept—a concept of a fake connection unbroken; the reward is a lie. In short, people can pay Snapchat to lie to themselves about their relationships with their friends. The only real gains are made by Snap Inc. in monetary value. Material relations between people and social relations between things, indeed.

Every time a user makes the choice to return to the social media marketplace—arguably is *compelled to*—the algorithm learns a nugget of information about a unique self that can be sold on the attention marketplace to bidders ranging from advertisers to governments. The services are not free: the users *"pay* attention" in exchange for accessing social media. In the social media marketplace, attention is a commodity that is exchanged in two forms of material relations between people. First, each user provides a unit of attention for a unit of time— say, twenty minutes of attention-time—to a social media company in exchange for social media access for the same unit of time. Second, the owners of the social media company exchange information or "data" gathered in the twenty minutes of attention-time to a third entity who is willing to exchange the given attention commodity unit for a desirable quantity of the money commodity. Through these two processes of exchange, the social media owner converts the attention of social media users into capital.

Let's briefly consider Marx's concepts of "use value," "exchange value," and "value" in the context of the social media marketplace. Marx notes: "The usefulness of a thing makes its use-value. But this usefulness does not dangle in mid-air.

It is conditioned by the physical properties of the commodity and has no existence apart from the latter."[14] Commodities have a use value because they serve a need. The need they serve is inseparable from the physical properties of the commodity. A bag of chips serves the need for sustenance. The owner of the chips cannot directly use it for sustenance without consuming its physical form. The owner of chips *can* indirectly use it for sustenance by exchanging the bag of chips with the owner of a loaf of bread. The owners of the chips and the bread meet at a marketplace and determine how many chips are equivalent to one slice of bread: the exchange value of each commodity. Chips and bread don't simply exist naturally, a human person exerts labor-power into existing ingredients to fry or bake them into consumables.

In his controversial labor theory of value, Marx argues that the *value* of each commodity is determined by the amount of labor-time that goes into producing it, all else being equal. Therefore, if one bag of chips requires three hours of labor-time, and one loaf of bread requires one hour of labor-time, one bag of chips is equivalent to three loaves of bread. The money commodity innovates in this process by introducing an agent whose use value is to expand itself so its owner can accumulate what essentially amounts to *power*. In order to do so, the owner needs a commodity that expands the value of disparate parts of other commodities: that special commodity is labor-power. When human workers provide mental and physical labor to a capitalist, the capitalist can, for example, convert a ten-dollar yarn to a fifty-dollar scarf. The scarf is made up of the cost of yarn and the cost of labor. The capitalist can maximize the "surplus value" of the scarf by minimizing the cost of labor. Without the capital to buy their own yarn, the laborer is forced to sell their labor-power to the capitalist to sustain their livelihood at whatever price the capitalist sets. The power dynamics between labor and capital are thus enshrined within a capitalist economic system that persistently favors the capitalist under the necessary conditions of exploitation of the laborer. It is beyond the scope of this book to debate the merits of the labor theory of value, which has been debated ad nauseam in the last few centuries.[15]

What remains relevant for the purposes of my argument is the undeniable existence of use values and surplus values. Commodities have physical properties that serve a desirable function for a given human being, and labor-power is a special commodity that supports the accumulation of surplus value.

Considering attention as a commodity leads to questioning it's use value. Attention lacks physicality outside of the physical body of its owner, the human person. The person has, keeps, or pays attention in units of time. As long as the person maintains a living body, the person has attention to pay, with time as the only boundary: *how much attention* could alternatively refer to quality of focus, which is not so easily measurable, leaving us with *how much time* is spent paying attention to a specific phenomenon or process.

To fully consume the use value of a bag of chips, the owner of chips must only eliminate any physical traces of the chips in the material plane. To fully consume the use value of one's attention, the owner of attention must be dead. Like with the commodity of labor-power, the owner of attention is inseparable from the use value of attention, the physical location of attention being the owner's living body. Yet attention as a commodity is also different from labor-power as a commodity. Labor-power is finite—eventually human beings reach a physical limitation where they can no longer supply this commodity without rest and replenishment. Attention, however, is *infinite* in living persons: even when people sleep, their consciousness is attentive to dreams and other subconscious phenomena. Thus, attention as a commodity is wholly inseparable from personhood. What is the use value of being a living person? There is no answer, nothing that can be measured with the tools of science or fully captured with the tools of language. We are here, toward whatever end, for whatever amount of time, until we die. We could be useful to so many people in so many ways, or we could be completely useless to anyone or anything depending on the time of day, present life context, and personal outlook. To the owner of attention, there is no use value of attention because the owner's physical body is inseparable from that person's mental focus even during periods of rest.

Miraculously for the ruling class, something without a concrete use value to its owner has an exchange value and value in the marketplace. Miraculously, *this use value dangles in midair*, for the physicality of the attention owner does not become fully consumed to materialize value. The physicality cannot be fully consumed in any living person. Attention is infinite and *unlimited*. Only *time is the limit*. Thus the algorithm is designed to increase the a*mount of time attention is paid toward a specific segment of the social media marketplace.* The capitalist entities that most successfully direct attention toward their platforms for the longest units of time derive the most value from the attention economy. The shadow-parasites that compel the most committed engagement from the largest number of hosts for the longest units of time can generate the most capital from the attention commodity: a miraculous commodity without exhaustible physicality. Such a commodity has the power to generate even more surplus value for the capitalist class than physical and material labor-power, which is exhaustible. The commodity is especially profitable in the attention economy where attention is not considered labor, and therefore *uncompensated.* The attention commodity is free for the capitalist and its supply is infinite, resulting in extraordinary gains in surplus value.

## LABOR AND THE ONLINE PROLETARIAT

Of labor and attention Marx writes: "The less [one] is attracted by the nature of the work and the way in which it has to be accomplished, and the less, therefore, he enjoys it as the free play of his own physical and mental powers, this closer his attention is to be[16] Here Marx makes the case that, capital generating labor or "work" demands complete attention to the task at hand, the quality of focus is inversely proportional to the level of enjoyment, and thus implicitly, work is necessarily separate from the enjoyable use of one's mental faculties and attention.

How does contributing to the attention economy constitute as labor? From the perspective of the attention-haver, internet use is a leisurely activity committed to enhance entertainment. ICTs are named such under an early, pre-Web 1.0 premise that the key function of these technologies would be distance communication and knowledge-sharing. Social media in Web 2.0 serves functions beyond distance communication and knowledge-sharing—although these key functions are also embedded within. For example, whenever I ask a room full of people ages eighteen to seventy to raise their hands if they learned about a recent world event from social media, 80 percent or more usually raise their hands. Nonetheless, more often than not, people log onto websites X, TikTok, and Reddit out of a need—often a *compulsive need*—for distraction. In other words, these websites provide ready-made containers for attention to flow into when the bearer of the attention is seeking an outlet. The algorithms underpinning these websites are designed to direct restless attention toward them whenever and wherever possible. In this way, the main function social media provides can be summed up loosely as "entertainment"—the socially desirable term for distraction.

Entertainment, of course, is not work because it is enjoyable. Furthermore, being online is not a form of labor because, in most cases, the user does not receive monetary compensation for the time spent supplying this attention. But closely observing some other ways in which Marx constructs the concepts of labor map on surprisingly well with the activity of being online.

First, let's consider time. Marx describes the value of a commodity as determined by "the amount of labor socially necessary, or the labor-time socially necessary for its production."[17] In other words, the value—i.e., capital generating potential—of a commodity depends on how much labor went into creating something that has use, the "how much" of labor itself is *measured* in the amount of time needed to create something of use. In the case of the attention economy, the value of the attention commodity is determined by the amount of time a user spends with a given algorithm providing attention capital. Here, time and attention are quantitatively but not qualitatively interchangeable. A user provides "twenty minutes of attention" to a social media platform. The amount of attention paid is quantitatively equal to the amount of time spent—note how it is the user who "spends" the time and "pays" the attention—so the commodity of interest is twenty minutes' worth of attention.

Qualitatively, however, those twenty minutes could be spent scrolling through devastating news about a major international crisis, reading fan fiction about a favorite fictional universe, or cyberbullying someone for using GMO ingredients in a recipe for soup. From the standpoint of capital accumulation, there is no distinction in the value produced by these qualitatively different forms of attention. Doomscrolling is equally valuable as rage bait, which is equally valuable as fan art: all forms of engagement contribute to an algorithm gaining an increasingly complex understanding of the multidimensional self: the attention commodity of interest. The *commodity*, of course, experiences these different forms of engagement differently in emotional capacity and in level of enjoyability. That might be true to some extent for industrial factory work in the factory system, but Marx dictates in clear terms that work, by design, is not supposed to be fun. Being online *is* fun. It is also devastating, joyful, rageful, lustful, unnerving, and captivating—sometimes all in one twenty-minute expenditure of time and attention. Notwithstanding the range of enjoyabilities—notably, enjoyable is different from *healthy*, which is covered in the next section— the user here provides attention-time that is converted into capital for the profit of another entity. In these ways, the attention economic system is different from the factory system in what constitutes work.

The other concepts to note here are "use value" and "socially necessary labor-time." I have covered use value, but it remains a difficult construct to unpack in the case of attention. The use value of human attention is to sustain personhood. When personhood is commodified, there is only surplus value, no "use" in terms of meeting societal needs. There is no social necessity that the process of whole-human commodification fulfills, only capital gains for the ruling class. Instead of socially necessary labor-time, *we consider capital generating attention-time*. Every person provides such attention-time when using the Web 2.0 mobile internet.

Yet they *volunteer* to do so because of perceived *enjoyability*, and except in the case of some successful "influencers," most people *pay* to volunteer (at a minimum for internet connection) rather than receive compensation.[18] Some platforms like TikTok do compensate users after they meet certain thresholds for virality—i.e., when they generate high levels of engagement from large numbers of users. Virality is completely uncertain and driven by algorithm in a mysterious fashion; thus, most people are unable to attain it. Even so, the fact that a minute fragment of TikTok users get paid encourages other users to spend hundreds of hours in creating content with the hopes of getting paid. As job prospects look increasingly bleak in the material economy, influencing appears as a viable alternative to sustain a livelihood—especially as people witness others succeed in this way. Most users remain uncompensated, but the content their labor generates nonetheless creates surplus-value for TikTok. Attaining virality is like winning the lottery, except winning the lottery does not require a tremendous expenditure of labor-power and attention.

In Marx's conception, capitalism is a unique system of economic exchange because it treats labor-power as a commodity. Labor-power is a *special* kind of commodity whose use value arises from its ability to expand the value of any commodity toward which labor-power is manifested as labor. Marx writes: "we mean by labor-power, or labor-capacity, the aggregate of those mental and physical capabilities existing in the physical form, the living personality, of a human being, capabilities which he sets in motion whenever he produces a use-value of any kind."[19] To simplify, labor-power spans all mental and physical qualities of being that go toward producing use values. Being online fits as such an expenditure of labor-power—until we get to the production of use values, where again we are forced to reckon with the online attention economy as a system that *surpasses social necessity in its reproduction.* There is no use of attention except the attention-haver's use of experiencing personhood and now the capitalist's use for exchange of the attention commodity. Exchange does take place; attention commodity is bought and sold in a marketplace of attention, and *value* is nonetheless generated for the capitalist trading in attention currency.

This value relies on "the physical form, the living personality, of a human being" in different ways than factory work, with an increased emphasis on personality and a decreased emphasis on physical form.

Thus far I have made the case that "being online" is a form of work because (1) the attention-time committed toward such activity is a profit-generating commodity regardless of the qualitative elements of that attention-time as experienced by the user, and (2) it is a form of labor-power—in the form of mental, emotional, and creative capacities—that is expended toward the generation of surplus value while surpassing traditional use value defined via social necessity.

Nonetheless, the work of being online is different from factory work for several reasons—for starters because factory work is quite obviously not fun.[20] First, the work of being online on Web 2.0 presents itself as a source of entertainment that does not feel in any way like labor. Second, most people are not paid for the work of being online. Capitalism exists as a system heralded for its "freedom" as a worker has the choice to exchange labor-power in the market for the money commodity, which allows the worker to continually exist by providing means of sustenance and other necessities. Marx argues that capitalists find a loophole in the system of freedom when they realize that they can purchase increasingly more labor-power for a steady amount of sustenance that is sufficient to cover enough labor necessary to maximize capital. In other words, the capitalist realizes labor can be exploited for evermore increasing gains. This nugget of unequal exchange between labor and capital then iterates toward all elements of market and society to create a social system in which power is concentrated among the capitalist ruling class.

Attention capitalism surpasses the need to provide subsistence entirely by swapping out money for payment via enjoyment, entertainment, clout, fun . . . different words for *distraction*. The unequal exchange occurs between attention-time supplied by the workers, and distraction received as payment. Power is concentrated among the owners of the means of distraction. This ruling class uses shadow-parasite algorithms to exploit the bearer of the attention commodity that supplies attention-time as the online proletariat.

The third distinction between factory work and the work of being online is that factory work explicitly discourages creative faculties for monotonous concentration toward a singular task. Marx notes that the quality of labor—skilled, unskilled, or otherwise—is not important in understanding how labor-power becomes value, as the entire process of exchange can be defined in terms of labor-time. For the attention economy, the quality of labor is critical because the attention commodity is extracted from the unique persona of each user. To do this successfully, the shadow-parasite needs to learn about the commodity at the deepest levels it can access: the creative self. Much of the work in the online attention economy is creative in nature, in direct contrast to factory work.

Creative activity is also not limited explicitly to "content creation"—which does cover large swaths of Web 2.0 online activity—but even constructing something as simple as a 240-word X post requires reason, creativity, and intellectual processing. In this way, online work allows us to consistently access our creative selves and honor, in theory, our species-being. Online work also allows us to share our work with others rather than trapping us in mundane task silos. These characteristics should, in theory, alleviate the alienation wrought by traditional labor and factory work. Yet in reality, alienation simply evolves. The unequal exchange between attention-time and distraction is lethal for the collective human spirit.

## ALIENATION AND SOCIAL REPRODUCTION OF THE ATTENTION ECONOMY

Capitalism is socially reproduced by increasing inequality and the concentration of wealth and capital in the hands of a minority ruling class who own the means of production and sustenance. The ruling class leverages ownership of the means of production to force workers to work in increasingly precarious conditions and for ever-decreasing wages. Because labor-time creates value in the Marxian sense, decreasing the cost of labor is always necessary to maximize profit and expand capital and power. The worker, lacking ownership to the means of sustenance, is increasingly desperate to meet the capitalist's demand to continue to exist, as well as to support any family and offspring. The capitalist has all the power to dictate the terms of exchange for the worker's time and labor-power, which the capitalist uses to ensure perpetually unequal exchange. To summarize: capitalism socially reproduces itself through the exploitation of workers to the benefit of owners.

In classical Marxian thought, this process of social reproduction through exploitation is only broken by workers expanding their collective power to violently overthrow the ruling class. Here, we run into another eternally debated Marxian construct beyond the scope of this book. As I have maintained so far, my goal is to demonstrate that the attention economy assumes characteristics of the materialist Marxian political economy but also emerges as something entirely novel: *a capitalist economic system that is different from the factory system.* The alienation that evolves under the attention economy is something different, indeed.

The concept of Marxist "alienation" is most commonly attributed to Marx's unpublished notes discovered in the early twentieth century and known as the "Economic and Philosophic Manuscripts of 1844." In these notes, Marx describes the product of any labor in capitalist production "as something alien, as a power independent of the producer." The use of the word "power" is critical here because Marx goes on to discuss at great lengths in his later works how wage labor enslaves humans to the commodities they produce, whose production determines the worker's ability for self-sustenance. Rather than invoking a sense of satisfaction that may arise from creating something, workers find that the product of their labor "confronts [the laborer] as something hostile and alien." In this way, under the capitalist mode of production, workers are alienated from the product of their labor, which assumes power over the workers' ability to exist.[21]

In the same manuscripts, Marx identifies three other forms of alienation. The worker is alienated from the task activity, the monotony failing to provide intrinsic rewards from the activity of creation. Workers are further alienated from their humanity, their "species-being," feeling themselves as being an alien entity stripped of the creative capacities that are rewarded to the unique human intellect. Finally, the worker is alienated from other human beings, who are themselves trapped into an alien process of creation independently of each other. These conceptions describe the labor process under the capitalist process as something innately inhumane, undignified, lonely, and alien. This is the very process whereby exchange adopts the "material relations between people, and social relations between things" model. In *Capital*, volume 1, Marx uses the term "commodity fetishism" to describe this process of commodity production stripping down human beings to production engines.

In the chapter on the working day of *Capital*, volume 1, Marx argues that the capitalist seeks to expand the working day to

stretch workers to their physical limits to ensure continual production of commodities. Per his earlier writings, this also indicates the capitalist seeks to sustain the sense of alienation for
much of workers' waking lives. Marx writes:

> the working day contains the full 24 hours, with the deduction
> of the few hours of rest without which labor-power is absolutely
> incapable of renewing its services. Hence, it is self-evident that
> the worker is nothing other than labor-power for the duration of
> his whole life, and therefore all his disposable time is by nature
> and by right labor-time, to be devoted to the self-valorization
> of capital. Time for education, for intellectual development, for
> the fulfillment of social functions, for social intercourse, for the
> free play of the vital forces of his body and his mind . . . what
> foolishness! But in its blind and measureless drive, its insatiable
> appetite for surplus labor, capital oversteps not only the moral but
> even the merely physical limits of the working day.[22]

He goes on to conclude that such overstepping of capital
repeatedly leads to "premature exhaustion and death of labor-
power itself." Marx is building the case that such an exploitation
cannot be sustained. Elsewhere he argues that such exploitation,
such deep alienation of being will result in worker solidarity and
a violent overthrow of the capitalist ruling class.[23]

Marx, of course, did not envision social media, where "labor-
time" and "time for education for intellectual development,
for the fulfillment of social functions, for social intercourse, for
the free play of the vital forces of his body and his mind" are
inexplicably the same. All of these characteristics are captured
by the "attention-time" through which capital is self-valorized.
*The method of capital accumulation in the attention economy is
an innovation against the destructive potentiality of unchecked*

*alienation*, in the traditional Marxian sense. The online proletariat is certainly granted unlimited time for "free-play."

No, unfettered—even toxic—devotion to play is critical for
the social reproduction of the attention economy.

In *Capitalist Realism: Is There No Alternative?*, Mark Fisher
uses the term "depressive hedonia" to describe a state of distress,
misery, and depression so pervasive yet so *productive*: "depression
is usually characterized as a state of anhedonia, but the condition
[described here] is constituted not by an inability to get pleasure
so much as it is by the inability to do anything else *except* pursue
pleasure. There is a sense that "something is missing"—but no
appreciation that the mysterious, missing enjoyment can only be
accessed *beyond* the pleasure principle."[24]

Fisher's concept of depressive hedonia comes closest to describing the state of despair that algorithmic shadow-parasites feed
on to perpetuate the attention economy (figure 1.1). It is no

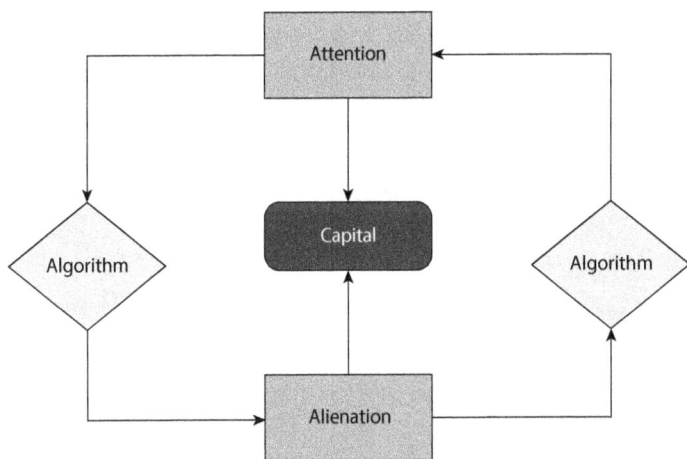

**FIGURE 1.1** The social reproduction of the attention economy.

longer necessary to force the continual expansion of the working day; the online proletariats are deceived by the continual dangling of the pleasure carrot in their face by advanced technologies designed to profit off their selfhood. Distraction for dependence, pleasure for data, fun for attention-time, and depressive hedonia for capital.

Unequal exchange, over and over and over again. Each algorithm suggests that the "something is missing" hole can be filled by directing one's attention to a specific app or service, and it's right. The hole is filled temporarily for a certain profitable bit of attention-time. Then the hole returns, and the user reaches for the phone, not fully present, not always aware of the act of reaching, always seeking to fill that hole, always searching for play. Without invoking and perpetuating such desperate addiction, the capitalist class is unable to ensure the voluntary expansion of the working day to every waking moment. Ingenious as the innovation is, the risk of premature death from overwork and exhaustion is no longer a concern for the capitalist in this attention economy, they have figured out a way to keep the worker commodity reaching and generating, even when material resources wane and life is reduced to the material relationship between each person and the person's smartphone. The commodity of attention has power over the person, even when the commodity *is inseparable from the person.* The commodity is not—cannot be—alien to self. The commodity and the self are inexplicably the same.

When the worker commodity experiences this form of alienation, it's no longer because they are unable to express their species-being but because they are forced to exhaust their creative capacities to generate data and capital. They are given a false sense of connection with others through social media, in material reality people are alone with their phones, looking for a way to fill the missing void, unaware that the phone is the void. Through completely contradictory mechanisms to Marxist alienation, the phone-object nonetheless reduces people to something inhumane, undignified, lonely, and alien. For alien is the body that houses the attention that provides attention-time to generate attention capital. Alien are the bodies of other people, who appear as two-dimensional creatures, as texts and images in the void, all providing attention-time to generate attention capital for the ruling class. Alien is the creative spirit, which may bring about a temporary sense of satisfaction only until the desire for social approval—through likes and reposts: newer and more innovating material relations between people—brings one right back to the attention marketplace, creating evermore content, posting evermore posts, hoping all the while for the body behind the phone to be seen, the despair acknowledged, the void filled.

To the ruling class in the attention economy, this kind of alienation is beyond simply profitable: this alienation serves to socially reproduce the attention economy. For in those moments when the attention commodities set down their phones and interact with other attention commodities in the material plane, capital is not generated for the attention economy. Meaningful social relationships between people—not things, not phones—reduce the working day. Activity and play outside of the digital marketplace reduces the working day. Even working in the traditional sense reduces this kind of working day, but the pleasure of the attention economy is so intoxicating that many people choose to work for the technological ruling class in the duration of their traditional working day. Workers may experience those stolen moments on their phones as a form of freedom or resistance from the traditional master, but in a twisted way, often they simply serve a different master.

Freedom does not exist within the attention economy. As long as the shadow-parasite is fed, it seeks more—more time, more attention, more clicks, more engagement—it seeks everything each person has to give in their human journey. The only way to freedom is putting the phone down and fighting the depressive hedonia it thrives on. Healing the self, healing each other, healing social relationships between people. Through the processes of healing it is possible to redirect individual and collective attention-time toward socially useful ends. It is even possible to create radical alternatives to the attention economy—Web 3.0 and beyond—that support collective well-being rather than dependence: online systems that work with offline social reality to actually fill the void. I return to healing and building new systems in chapter 5.

For now, I conclude this section with the contention that healing serves similar functions in the attention economy as a violent overthrow of the ruling class may serve in the material economy. Alienation in the attention economy is profitable; therefore, to overcome underlying despair by whatever means possible and regain power over one's own attention-time—as Jenny Odell also previously concluded—is a revolutionary act.

## WORLD ATTENTION ECONOMIC SYSTEM

How does the attention economy reproduce across the boundaries of nation-states? As cyberoptimists of years past—not excluding myself in this band of naïve hopefuls of yore—have been keen to note, the internet is borderless! Before the successful monetization of the World Wide Web, before a thriving attention economy, before the Telecommunications Act of 1996, there was hope. Hope that the democratization of knowledge, the digital abolition of borders, and the revolution in instant communications would teach everyone in the world all that is right and true to set humanity on a path of a victorious collective future of egalitarianism, education, and democracy. I do not negate these potentialities even today—for this is not a book for the easily despaired—but so far they have been exploited by a variety of international agents to push for the expansion of the attention economy toward the Global South.

Even as the World Wide Web changed thoroughly between Web 1.0 and Web 2.0, the language of information and communications technology for development (ICT4D) remained largely unchanged. Proponents of ICT4D sparsely engaged with the revolutionary transition between Web1.0 and Web 2.0 that led to a thriving economy of attention that is inherently exploitative. With exceptions, ICT4D discourse remains focused on the promises of democracy and freedoms, as though trading in human attention does not negate the possibility of freedom for those whose attention are stolen.[25] When development agents support the expansion of ICTs as they stand today, they inadvertently support the expansion of the pool of the human population whose attention is exploited for the process of capital accumulation for the ruling class. Under the premise of development, increasingly larger segments of Global South populations are integrated into what I describe as "the world attention economic system."

The concept of the world attention economic system derives from the neo-Marxian global theory of world-systems analysis. World-systems scholars undertake what is known as the *longue duree* approach to studying political economy.[26] These neo-Marxist scholars are concerned with understanding global change over long periods of the history of capitalism. The world historical perspective of world-systems analysis treats the world as a single unit of interconnected economic activities. Nation-states are a collection of geographical units that engage with one another via trade and the capitalist world economy. This single capitalist system is divided into three different zones based on their relative economic and productive capacities. These zones are the core, the periphery, and semi-periphery states. Crudely, core states are postindustrial regions of the world into which the majority of revenue generated by global capitalism flows.[27] These states have moved away from industrial production and operate as knowledge economies that sell ideas rather than material goods.

The United States is an ideal example of a core state, and it also serves as the present global hegemon: essentially the ruling nation controlling the capitalist world economy. In the *longue durée* of global capitalism (i.e., five hundred or so years of post-feudalist society), there has been a hegemonic transition every century or so during critical periods of transition and global change. For example, after World War II, the United States replaced the British Empire as the hegemonic core.[28]

Periphery states are regions of the world that are industrializing and providing cheap labor and natural resources to facilitate capitalist production. These states also experience the most adverse effects of continual industrial production, including pollution and environmental catastrophe. Nepal, for example, serves a peripheral state under a world-systems framework. Semi-periphery refers to a small number of states that engage both corelike and periphery economic processes. China and India are two semi-peripheral states that are presently competing for the status of the next global hegemon as we approach the theoretical close of the century of U.S. domination in the political economy.[29]

World-systems analysis is primarily concerned with how global capitalism influences the politics and economics of core, periphery, and semi-periphery states. As economic globalization in the form of neoliberalism expands, multinational corporations (MNCs) populate peripheral and semi-peripheral zones, exporting industrial activity and exploiting cheaply available labor and resources. Such a relationship of exploitation between the core and the periphery has adverse consequences, including environmental destruction, resource exhaustion, and rapidly expanding economic inequality in periphery states.

The world capitalist system cannot exist without exploiting the periphery to extract wealth for core countries. The necessary relationship of exploitation poses a real challenge for the system in its current state and in this period in history. The project of endless capital accumulation has thus far relied on extracting natural and material resources from the Earth, particularly in periphery countries. As we live and experience unprecedented environmental destruction and global climate change, it becomes increasingly apparent that continued capital accumulation through such resource exploitation is not sustainable.[30] In sociology, such unsustainability is predicted by the theory of the "treadmill of production," which posits that capitalist societies that emphasize endless capital accumulation will experience extreme levels of ecological destruction that is incompatible with further capital accumulation.[31]

The *world attention economic system* is one of the ways the world capitalist system is currently adapting to the contradiction between capital accumulation and ecological collapse (figure 1.2). Because natural and material resources are rapidly depleting, the world-system is adapting by generating new sources of wealth. The attention economy is a premiere source of wealth that does not directly rely on natural resources— although indirectly, physical devices and cloud storage both rely on excessive use of material resources leading to extreme

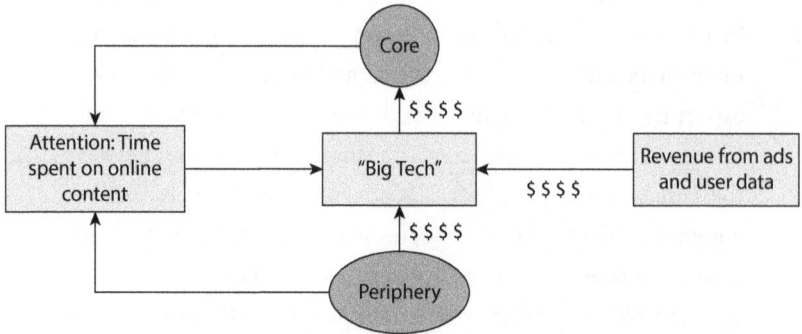

FIGURE 1.2  The world attention economic system.

*Source:* Previously published in the *Journal of World Systems Research* and reproduced here under their open access policy and creative commons license.

events such as mass deaths in the Democratic Republic of Congo due to conflicts over the mineral Coltan that is used in the production of smartphones. Though these material exploitations are ongoing and exacerbated by the technological ruling class, they have also innovated immaterial forms of exploitation in the attention economy.

A key innovation by "big tech" companies that spearhead the attention economy is rendering the consumer of ICTs, and particularly social media, as the product that generates wealth. Peoples' psychology, behaviors, hopes, dreams, and fears are monitored, so algorithms can generate content that captures their attention, keeping them online. Their online patterns of behavior—what they pay attention to—are then bought and sold as data that can generate further wealth for powerful technology corporations such as Meta Inc. and Apple Inc. Some of the largest big tech MNC firms are based in the hegemonic core of the United States, and they facilitate increased wealth for the United States even against a materially depleting Earth.

When *semi-periphery* states threaten the core's hegemonic control of the attention economy, the core retaliates, which is plain in the example of the TikTok platform. At the time of this writing, TikTok is among the most profitable social media platforms that owns the most sophisticated shadow-parasite algorithm technology in existence.[32] Headquartered in the semi-periphery state of China, ByteDance Ltd. has access to massive amounts of data that have great value in the attention market-place. In April 2024, the U.S. president Joe Biden signed the Protecting Americans from Foreign Adversary Controlled Applications Act that requires either a ban or forced sale of the under-lying propriety algorithm from ByteDance to a U.S. company.[33] Subsequently, as U.S. companies such as Microsoft and Oracle consider purchasing TikTok in this process, recent estimates suggest that the TikTok application as a whole is worth $100 billion.[34] The same sources indicate that without the underlying pro-prietary algorithm, the value of the application drops to $30 to $40 billion. The value of the algorithm itself is estimated at 60 to 70 billion U.S. dollars. Although the Chinese company is challenging the bill through the U.S. court system, the *value* of a particularly sophisticated shadow-parasite in the world atten-tion economy is elucidated by the TikTok case. The hegemonic core uses its power to maintain control over the highly profitable attention economy and the capital it generates, thwarting semi-periphery attempts to compete by any means necessary.

Notably, exploitation of the periphery is a necessary condition for the capitalist world-system to continue. As ICT access spans across the periphery and more people in Global South countries are online, the attention economy can massively expand capital accumulation without too much reliance on natural and mate-rial resources. In the same way that material economies exploit Global South populations to generate wealth for core countries, the attention economy exploits Global South populations to generate wealth for core countries. Unintentionally or otherwise, ICT4D and the development status quo supports exploitation of Global South populations for wealth generation in the core.

In the next two chapters, I argue that ICT4D is yet another way to support the ruling class agenda in the realms of international development. Traditional development supported expansion of foreign aid and structural adjustment so MNCs could extract wealth from the periphery. Modern, ICT-based development is doing the exact same thing so big tech companies can extract wealth from the periphery. ICT4D is simply old development in a new iPhone. Then, in chapter 4, I focus on the mesolevel of social movements and counter movements as they take place within the attention economy. Finally, I unpack the individual level implications in chapter 5 before highlighting some concluding remarks.

# INTERLUDE 1

## BASKIN-ROBBINS IN KATHMANDU

This story involves me going out for ice cream at a Baskin-Robbins with some extended family members and family friends. I was nine years old at the time, old enough to recognize that going out to get ice cream from a global chain in the trendy neighborhood of Durbar Marg (translated to and sometimes referred to as "King's Way") was a unique, polished, Western activity. The overwhelming majority of Nepali children could not even conceptualize such a foreign and exquisite luxury. Many adults I accompanied were highly educated Nepali elites who worked with foreign aid in the development sector. They socialized with Western development workers and traveled abroad often enough to have absorbed Western cultural traditions.

The degree to which this act of getting ice cream was a normalized part of their (our) everyday lives symbolized how detached our lives were from most Nepalis. Around the turn of the millennium you had to be of a certain class and social status to casually patronize any business in Durbar Marg. Only two kinds of people usually walked this single strip of road alongside the Narayanhiti Palace, the official national home of the monarchy. Aside from the kinds of people I was with—those who went to Baskin Robins—the road was populated with children and sometimes adults who hoped the wealthy and foreign or foreign-adjacent clientele would be good targets for begging.

Based on my personal experience, that strategy never appeared to be particularly successful. The wealthiest and most cosmopolitan Nepalis rarely gave money to begging children. When we left Baskin Robins that afternoon—each with our unique selection of one among twenty-one delicious flavors of international ice cream—we were surrounded by children begging for money or food or whatever they could get their hands on. The adults in my crew began scolding these kids and yelling at them for sniffing glue (a common stereotype about begging street children in Kathmandu, even though some of these kids were younger than I was). I looked around at my little cousins—future elites sure to join the next generation of folks in the development sector—and saw them protecting their ice creams for dear life.

As for me, I made a huge mistake that I would be scolded about for days to come. I gave one of the begging kids my ice cream. I didn't even want it that much. I will never forget the ride home that day: my fancy aunts and cousins berated me for my atrocious behavior. I would not be invited along for ice cream next time. When we got home, my mom was informed, and she looked red in the face. When everyone left she said to me: "I understand why you did that, but why did you have to do it in front of *them*?"

The point of the story is not to emphasize how I was a more empathetic kid than the adults around me, because there are plenty of stories I could share in which I was complicit in the cruel and abhorrent treatment of folks from oppressed classes and castes. That kind of treatment of people was so normative when I was growing up that it is difficult to separate it from the heavily polluted air we breathed and continue to breathe in Kathmandu today. My mother was annoyed with me because mindlessly giving the begging children some ice cream was deemed a radical act of norm violation by the people I was accompanying. These were the people everyone in my community looked up to, admired, and desired to emulate: the fancy foreign educated folks working with the UN or some international nongovernmental organization. Apart from designing and implementing development programs as they saw fit, they also determined what was culturally acceptable and wrote the rules of conduct for my society.

Their rules explicitly forbade acts of kindness toward those less fortunate than themselves. This point is worth taking some time to process. In my experience growing up among the elites of Nepal, the people managing development at their core denied the humanity of the people they claimed to serve. These people, who were taking on large sums of foreign aid under the guise of improving the livelihoods of the most destitute populations of the country, loathed the poor (rather than poverty). Such an attitude is built into the fabric of Nepalese society, so I can't blame it all on imperialism without first addressing the issues of caste. With Western imperialism came a new and lasting form of stratification, but the foundation around which the entire project was built and sustained itself—at least in South Asian societies and particularly in Nepal—lies in the Hindu caste system.

# 2

# ICT4D, UNEQUAL EXCHANGE, AND NEOLIBERAL IMPERIALISM

G lobal sociologists draw from the world-systems perspective to engage the concept of "unequal exchange," that describes a system of global relations that present as relations of exchange between core and periphery nations, and that upon close examination unveil exploitative dynamics.[1] Many studies about unequal exchange between core and periphery nations emphasize health and environmental outcomes, arguing that in the processes of international trade with core countries periphery populations often receive adverse health effects and ecological damage.[2] In many cases, these unequal and adverse effects are the consequences of the project of "development," a concept with many definitions—as I argue throughout this chapter—that all in some capacity invoke neoliberal capitalism and Western imperialism.

Information and communications technologies for development (ICT4D) foster unequal exchanges at two levels. First, at the level of expanding the attention economy, ICT4D programs push to present Global South populations with new information and communications functions at the cost of their attention and user data. Second, at the level of functioning as another development agenda, ICT4D reinforces the neoliberal and imperial premise of development: as discussed extensively, for example, in Firuzeh Shokooh Valle's book *In Defense of Solidarity and Pleasure: Feminist Technopolitics in the Global South*.[3] In this chapter, I first argue that ICT4D promotes technologically unequal exchange. I then describe the history of development and development agents to underscore how most development projects—spearheaded under the leadership of the United Nations—have their historical basis in Western neoliberal imperialism. I outline the history of modern developmentalism along with a broad range of literatures that demonstrate how development itself is a form of unequal exchange.

## TECHNOLOGICALLY UNEQUAL EXCHANGE

When developing populations access ICTs, they acquire new abilities, such as the ability to communicate instantaneously and to access any information immediately. It is difficult to deny the utility of these revolutionary communication features. The undeniable utility of ICTs is perhaps why there is a robust academic and policy focus on making these technologies available to a wide global population. There are increasingly critical ICT4D approaches that recognize the potential harms of an outdated concept of development and suggest reframing ICT4D around matters of justice.[4] I add to these studies by arguing that the attention economy *renders the use of the technology itself unequal*, beyond the problematic nature of the development premise—before reiterating the problematic nature of the development premise.

At the center of my argument is the premise that Global South populations are like Global North populations in how they use ICTs: they primarily use smartphones and the internet to access social media.[5] The GSMA organization has more than

one thousand mobile phone operators globally, and their reports
of mobile phone use across Global South countries consistently
demonstrate that the majority of people use mobile phones primarily for social media access.[6]

Figure 2.1 shows patterns of mobile usage across twenty-
seven Global South countries using the most recently available

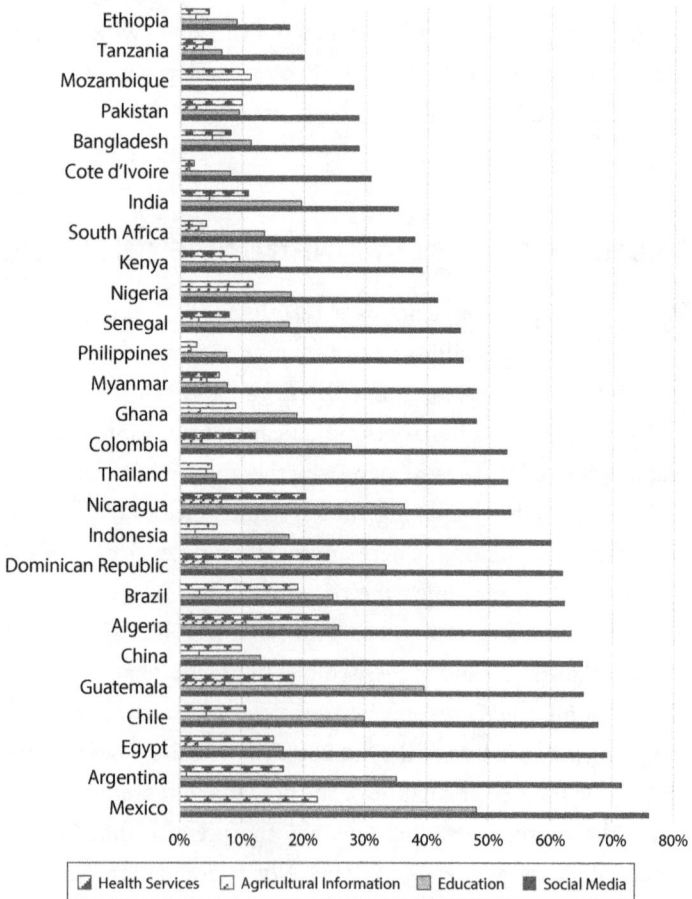

FIGURE 2.1 Mobile phone use across twenty-seven Global South countries.

GSMA data. Social media use consistently ranks as the most popular way to use mobile phones in each of the twenty-seven countries, with education often serving the second most popular use but trailing far behind social media in most cases. It is clear from these patterns that social media use is the most popular utility of mobile phones in these countries. Social media use does not negate other—arguably more empowering—usage such as education or accessing health information, of course. At the same time, social media use *ensures* that people using mobile phones are performing labor for the technological ruling class because most popular social media websites trade user data in the attention economy.

On the one hand, as more people in the Global South use mobile phones, ICT4D proponents argue that they experience some new abilities, including accessing health information, educational support, and more.[7] The benefits of such expanded utilities are certainly numerous. For example, in rural parts of Global South countries where access to hospitals and health posts are severely limited, mobile health services that send Short Message Service (SMS) information about disease prevention can be life-saving for many people.[8] Likewise, farmers are able to better monitor weather patterns and access easy extension services.[9] These are some tangible benefits of the utility functions provided by ICT expansion.

On the other hand, as more people in the Global South use mobile phones, big tech companies such as Meta Platforms Inc. and Google LLC. acquire a larger segment of the population whose attention they can buy and sell as data in the open market. Whenever users connect with "free" services such as social media or streaming videos, their behavior and attention become a commodity sold by the social media companies who own these services. Without the expansion of supply in the attention commodity market, the companies that buy and sell attention fail to continuously generate revenue and capital. Thus the expansion of ICTs across the Global South is extremely beneficial to the big tech industry.

Is the commodification of one's personhood a fair price to pay for the ability to access new functions and services? I argue that this is a form of *technologically unequal exchange*. Ecologically unequal exchange refers to the phenomenon in which "development" via economic growth and infrastructural expansion leads to environmental catastrophes and has a disproportionate impact on climate change in Global South countries.[10] I make the case for technologically unequal exchange in a similar way: Global South populations receive some form of developmental expansion, but in exchange they experience an exploitation of their very identities and selfhoods, and the commodification of their attention. These populations perform mental and emotional labor that is uncompensated to generate capital for big tech firms, often to the detriment of the population's mental and emotional well-being.[11] This exchange feels even more unequal when considering the relative use for social media compared to other usages (figure 2.1).

Not only is this process of labor and capital uncompensated, *but the users also must pay money to buy into their own exploitation.* Even though a lot of these services are free in exchange for user data, people need to spend money to buy smartphones, and the cost of maintaining a networked service is ongoing. In this way, any utility accessed through these devices is a utility that people pay for, and corporations make money on both ends—from selling the phones as well as from selling the user data.

The development utilities people pay for access to are also imperfect. For example, in our 2023 study my coauthor (Burroway) and I found that women's education moderated the success of mobile health programs for preventing new HIV infections across seventy-six Global South countries over nearly three decades.[12] In other words, mobile phones are only helpful for HIV prevention when formal schooling rates for women are low; when women's education reaches higher levels, mobile phone access has no effect. In this way, ICTs do not mitigate the need for systemic changes and government intervention to expand educational access. Similarly, in their 2020 Sri Lanka study, Lim et al. also found that ICTs have the possibility to support educational efforts only when they are *systematically* integrated into existing curriculum.[13]

In each case, government intervention to support systemic freedoms takes precedence over the utility tool, which serves as a potential means rather than an end. Neoliberal capitalism opposes governmental intervention, and development often takes the shape of neoliberal capitalism. This results in a paradox in which development is unable to meet its stated goals. Moreover, as decades of research consistently show, development itself is a type of paradox, one that mines the exploitation of the very population it aims to serve.

## GLOBAL INSTITUTIONS AND INTERNATIONAL DEVELOPMENT

Growing up in Nepal it was communally understood that engagement with the United Nations signaled elite status. Most people were aware that the UN as well as many INGOs came to our country for "development" initiatives. They were here to fix our water systems, expand education in rural areas, and help us with our flailing infrastructure. Much of Kathmandu is still waiting for those improved water systems. A form of cognitive dissonance that many people I knew practiced was accepting—sometimes revering—the premise of development but understanding the fact that concrete changes never arrived for the majority. Meanwhile, my social position as a Kathmandu elite constantly exposed me to the foreign-educated, cosmopolitan, upper-stratum of Nepalese society who were *thriving* as a result of these organizations operating in our country. They accessed exclusive employment opportunities within these organizations, earned exorbitant salaries, traveled around the world, and received massive subsidies to send their children to elite universities abroad. That was my view of the UN and INGOs as an adolescent: they were in my country to address the grim and gritty realities of extreme poverty and material depravation, and their local employees were so cosmopolitan: so *fancy*.

What I didn't understand then, but over a decade of scholarship on international development has taught me, is that "development" is a weak and hollow concept. Civil society organizations such as the UN and various INGOs worked alongside academics for decades after World War II to present "development" as a viable—if not the *only*—approach to reform the Global South.[14] Major global institutions were to collectively design development agendas, which would ultimately solve absolute poverty, global inequality, and material depravation for the majority of the world.[15]

Integrated deeply within the 2030 sustainable development goals (SDGs)—the central UN program from which most contemporary development programs trickle down—ICT4D is the latest iteration of civil society's attempts to save the Global South using innovative technological solutions.[16] Tracing the origins of international development programs helps to further contextualize the neoliberal imperialism inherent in ICT4D.

## UNITED NATIONS MDGS, SDGS, AND ICT4D

The harbinger of modern internationalism, the UN's key role in the twenty-first century global order involves determining blueprints for progress and "development." The first development agenda of this magnitude, the millennium development goals (MDGs), was born after the 2000 Millennium Summit in New York City. At this summit, world leaders came together to discuss this pressing question: *What do we say the UN does in the new millennium?*[17] The MDGs exemplified the broad-brush development strategy to the UN Millennium Declaration's political resolution, which was signed by 189 countries at the UN General Assembly in 2000. For the next fifteen years, all development initiatives were focused on meeting these specific goals, which have faced tremendous criticism for reasons including but not limited to (1) uneven progress between nations with different income levels due to analytical incompetency, i.e., the objectives, some scholars note, were chosen seemingly at random.[18] (2) Western hegemony, i.e., the MDGs were designed to increase Global South countries' reliance on Western nations.[19] And (3) an underemphasis on within-country inequality beyond issues of gender empowerment.[20] Although certain developing populations experienced some improvements in absolute poverty and health care access, MDGs have largely failed to live up to the explicit and overzealous promise of completely eradicating extreme poverty and hunger.[21] Even with fifteen years of concentrated civil society efforts, the vast majority of development aid moving around in this time, and the influential support of their intellectual brand ambassador Jeffery Sachs, the MDGs still failed to produce the desired results. Confounded, the leaders of the world and the UN General Assembly moved in the only direction they understood with regard to change: reform the reform agenda! A nice reform of the MDGs would certainly fill the missing gaps and lead us, at long last, to the elusive state of "no poverty" and "zero hunger" in the world.[22] These are the first and second items in the follow-up sustainable development goals (SDGs). To be attained by 2030, the sibling to the MDGs now reigns over most development projects and platforms active today.

The SDGs differ from the MDGs in a few relatively minor ways. Most notably, they boast an explicit emphasis on environmental sustainability, taking center stage in the very title of the project. Such emphasis was in direct response to some of the more damning criticisms of the MDGs for failing to appropriately address environmental concerns.[23] In classic General Assembly fashion, they were all too eager to shift the presentation of their agendas to a more palatable version from a public relations standpoint.

The other key new feature of the SDGs lies at the heart of this book. SDG 9 focuses on industry, innovation, and infrastructure: to "build resilient infrastructure, promote inclusive and sustainable industrialization, and foster innovation."[24] How, in the twenty-first-century attention economy, does one *foster these innovations*? Target 9c provides us with the incisive answer: by ensuring that everyone in the world has access to ICTs.

The target is to "significantly increase access to information and communications technology and strive to provide universal and affordable access to the Internet in least developed countries by 2020."[25] They are specifically focused on the indicators measuring the percent of global mobile phone subscriptions, and the percent of people in the world with internet access. At the time of this writing, 2020 has come and gone, and some of the poorest developing populations have suffered the burdens of isolation in this pandemic ridden world without any access to mobile phones or the internet.[26] The point, for now, is that there is little reason to expect change to materialize in the Global South just because the General Assembly declares a development goal with a deadline.

In other words, I want to emphasize the *symbolic* nature of all UN General Assembly commitments and their historical origins. The fascinating history of the UN more broadly, but the General Assembly specifically, is simultaneously colonial and anticolonial.[27] Credited as the humanitarian, equitable wing of the UN as well as the first international body to promote the voices of leaders from the third world, the General Assembly has managed the UN's reputation from the start. For example, the 2000 Millennium Forum simply served as an avenue for the UN to meet and determine their roles and futures in the world in the twenty-first century. According to the historian Mark Mazower in his book *No Enchanted Palace: The End of Empire and the Ideological Origins of the United Nations*, such self-evaluation and search for purpose is a historically routine practice for the organization. Fluidity and reinvention mark key characteristics of the UN that developed after 1946. But this flexibility does not quite depict the principles and premises under which this organization was founded.[28]

## A BRIEF HISTORY OF
## THE UNITED NATIONS

The founding conference for the UN in 1945 in San Francisco was a controversial gathering, and many national delegates abandoned the event for sending hypocritical messages. Mazower writes: "they saw its universalizing rhetoric of freedom and rights as all too patrial—a veil masking the consolidation of a great power directorate that was not as different from the Axis powers, in its imperious attitude to how the world's weak and poor should be governed, as it should have been."[29] Such critiques were not surprising, given that the most influential figure in writing the UN preamble was the South African segregationist, white nationalist settler-leader, and apartheid proponent Jan Smuts.[30] In spite of the colonial intentions Smuts set for the new UN, W. E. B. DuBois was among the only intellectuals to challenge his involvement at the time.[31] Heavily involved in the UN's establishment, Smuts envisioned the organization as a postwar extension and effective rebranding of the League of Nations that existed between 1920 and 1946. Created after World War I, the league was the first intergovernmental organization (IGO) in the history of internationalism. In the most literal sense, it created modern internationalism characterized by national member state participation in global institutions. Many of the original founders of the UN saw it as a clear extension of the first iteration, with key imperial ideological functions expected to continue.[32]

The league's key mission was to maintain world peace after the turbulent war, and it also focused on issues of human rights, global health, and settling territorial disputes between nations.[33] Some of the major differences between the modern-day UN and the league were that the league was much smaller, much whiter, and quite overtly colonial. Mazower best summarizes the characteristics of the premiere global institution: "The League itself was an eminently Victorian institution, based on the notional superiority of the great powers, an instrument for global civilizing mission through the use of international law and simultaneously a means of undergirding British imperial world leadership and cementing its partnership with the United States."[34]

Unfortunately for the British Empire's mission to civilize what they saw as lesser, darker, and primitive nations, the United States could only join the subsequent iteration of the global institution known as the United Nations. In some ways, the UN was formulated for purposes of attracting the United States. Specifically, the UN conducted the delicate political function of bringing the three Allied powers of the United States, Great Britain, and the Soviet Union into the same room for a peace accord. To ascertain this tricky victory, the veto was invented, ceding ultimate power to the permanent members of the Security Council, which includes the three Allies, France, and only one predominantly nonwhite nation, China. Although the General Assembly operates separately from the Security Council—and deals with matters most relevant to this chapter, that is, development agendas—the veto power integrated into the formulation of the Security Council clearly outlines which nations are at the top of the international hierarchy. For example, the power imbalances produced by such clear hierarchies entrenched within the UN are visible in 2024 in how the United States consistently uses its veto power to prevent a ceasefire against an ongoing brutal genocide in Palestine. The United States is consistently the only country to disagree with a ceasefire within the security council—with Switzerland and the UK abstaining—and it has the ability to single-handedly ensure the genocide continues.[35]

Maintenance of these firm hierarchies was crucial from the standpoint of early UN founders such as Jan Smuts. Smuts saw the UN as an opportunity to have his cake and eat it too: continue the imperial civilization mission under white leadership and also convince the United States to grab a seat at the table. Smuts was not the only white supremacist to be involved in the UN's original establishment. The first ever Secretary General of the UN, Trygve Lie of Norway, saw Great Britain as an exemplary

force to lead lesser member states into the new dawn of civilization. In spite of his reverence for the British Empire, Lie has
somehow garnered a historical reputation as an important anticolonial figure in the ideological development of the UN. This
was the result of his occupying the Secretary General role during
the period of the great South African–Indian dispute between
1945 and 1955. In this period, the General Assembly evolved as
the anticolonial, antiracist wing of the UN.

The General Assembly, overall, boasts a more empowered
narrative of third world self-determination, especially when compared to the overt colonial hierarchies of the Security Council.
However, a closer look at the historical and contemporary activities of the assembly demonstrates glaring blind spots regarding
within-country oppression that is symptomatic of the nation-
alistic ideologies entrenched in modern global institutions. For
example, scholars see the great dispute between South Africa
and India, this decade-long conflict, as the tipping point when
the UN left behind the imperial legacies of its predecessor and
became an entirely new kind of institution; one that provides
a platform for Global South countries to challenge colonialism
and promote anticolonialism.[36]

The conflict actually involved Jan Smuts, who was disappointed to find that the white supremacist IGO of his creation
would eventually turn on him and censure him for continuing
an apartheid state in South Africa. As one of the last remaining countries to engage in state-sanctioned racial discrimination,
South Africa received both support and opposition from various
UN member states. Secretary General Lie himself was empathetic to Sumts's position when the Indian government, led by
Jawaharlal Nehru, unexpectedly asked to enter South Africa's
maltreatment of Indians on the agenda for the first ever General Assembly meeting. This set off both a decade-long dispute

between delegates of these two nations at this forum and the tradition of invoking the General Assembly to address matters of racial discrimination, and subsequently human rights and international development.

India's ultimate victory, which led to the condemnation of South Africa, was a symbolic transformation of the UN's internationalism from imperialist to cosmopolitan, global, and *equitable*. This is the dominant narrative among scholars about the UN's emergence as a forum for anticolonial struggle, and it is *fair enough*. Strictly speaking, it represents an accurate history of events that transpired between a dominant nation and the members of an oppressed nation that fought against discrimination. From the point of view of nationalist internationalism—the brand that started the concept in the mid-ninetieth century and dominates today—the UN emerged as a champion for the dispossessed by the time the South Africa and Indian dispute was "settled," symbolically as it may have been. South Africa got a stern scolding, and this was the first time members of a colonized nation were able to hold a settler nation accountable in a global forum.

## CASTE HIERARCHIES: THE OTHER SIDE OF THE GREAT INDIA–SOUTH AFRICA DEBATE

What many scholars gloss over in the heartwarming story of Indian victory is that Indian migrants were a small proportion of the oppressed groups in South Africa facing discrimination in this time. The moral leader of the Indian community there and everywhere, Mohandas Karamchand Gandhi, was heavily involved in persuading Nehru to bring the issue of discrimination against Indians to the General Assembly floor.

It was really his idea, supported by Nehru and expertly executed to perfection by a woman named Vijaya Laxmi Pandit.[37] An important question that is often overlooked in the historical retelling of this General Assembly victory is this: *What was Gandhi really mad about?*

As a dominant-caste leader, Gandhi was a proponent of preserving the caste system in India. A vocal opponent of dismantling the caste system, Gandhi envisioned dominant castes as representing the great *Aryan* race, equal in every way to the white race.[38] For someone who is globally acclaimed for defeating imperialism in India, Gandhi had an almost shocking level of commitment to both maintaining hierarchies and securing himself dominant positions within those hierarchies. No wonder he was quite fond of the segregationist Smuts and gave specific instructions to Pandit about being delicate toward him on the General Assembly floor: "Mrs. Pandit was to remember that Smuts was 'a man of God', and she was to shake his hand and 'ask your blessing for my cause.'"[39]

During the time he lived in South Africa, Gandhi was enraged to find that his dominance was not accepted in the apartheid state.[40] He saw himself and the white powers in South Africa as Aryan brethren, but they did not see him that way at all. No, he was simply insulted to find that they saw him as equal with the *kafir*, his preferred derogatory slur for the Black folks living under the South African apartheid state.

When matters of racial discrimination were brought to the floor of the UN General Assembly at the behest of Gandhi, it focused entirely on the treatment of Indians: the Aryan equals to the whites, from his perspective. South Africa was ultimately reprimanded only for human rights transgressions against Indians, and the subjugation and discrimination against Black communities continued in an apartheid that did not end until 1991.

There was little discussion of discrimination against Black South Africans in the General Assembly hearing. The conversation was about discrimination, but only a specific kind of discrimination against a group that occupied elite status in their country of origin. The historical antiracist victory of the General Assembly was, in a lesser understood sense, also the victory of a dominant group in successfully separating themselves as superior to the races at the bottom of the hierarchy.

Global power and national power merged to formulate this new internationalism that carries both the imperial legacies of its predecessor, the League of Nations, and a very specific version of human rights rhetoric that all too often promotes the agendas of national elites. And *rhetoric*, rather than meaningful action, is what most of UN General Assembly activity really boils down to. Such is the legacy that ultimately gave rise to the global development initiatives MDGs, SDGs, and ICT4D.

ICT4D is a great contemporary example of symbolic change perpetuated by the United Nations. As Valle describes in her book *In Defense of Solidarity and Pleasure*, the ICT4D platform is designed to invoke, for example, the symbol of "the third world technological woman." A type of woman that Valle argues cannot exist outside of the symbolic construction of the development status quo: someone who overcomes systemic injustices by using technology to boost a new innovative business, boost the livelihood of people she takes care of in her feminine role, and boosts the economy of her nation. None of these symbols invoke a woman struggling with body image issues due to excessive social media exposure, or in Valle's example, women experiencing disproportionate sexual harassment on the internet. These latter examples are often the reality of Global South people trapped in the attention and alienation cycle, whereas the UN and development agents tell a completely different story.

## A WORLD CULTURE OF DEVELOPMENT

Of course, to really understand the concept of "development" it is insufficient to delve into the history of the UN General Assembly that conducts the function of creating some of the major mainstream development agendas such as ICT4D. IGOs such as the UN are one aspect of what some scholars call the "world polity."[41] Scholars of the world polity identify global civil society networks as trendsetters and changemakers across countries and over time, especially in relation to matters of governance, human rights, and development.[42] First proposed by the Stanford sociologists Meyer, Boli, and Thomas, this framework posits a global network of actors and agents who carry and transmit civil society cultural norms as designated "scripts" across countries. These scripts are determined by a global network of IGOs via conferences, conventions, resolutions, and treaty ratifications. Nations plugged into these IGO networks symbolically cosign agenda scripts (relative to concepts of human rights and development) that determine the structure and quality of "progress."[43] Collectively, nations accept IGO standards as universal standards. The most well-known example of these standards is perhaps the Universal Declaration of Human Rights designed by the UN and ratified by forty-eight participating nations in 1948. Development programs such as the MDGs and SDGs are more recent examples of similar broad-stroke universalization of collective progress. ICT4D is a contemporary development script in world society, thus is it at the center of so many development initiatives across countries.

There is an inspiring volume of empirical research conducted by global sociologists on the topic of the world polity since the late 1990s. This work is currently ongoing, but scholarship on this topic has approached consensus around certain ideas. One key consensus is that the world polity works with what is known as the "world society" to create a "world culture" with its own sets of norms, values, agendas, and practices.[44] Whereas world polity indicates the network of nations embedded within leading global IGOs for agenda setting around progress, world society refers to the network of international nongovernmental organizations (INGOs) that promote stated world polity agendas among citizens within countries.[45] Together these civil society institutions curate and transmute "world culture": a globalized series of laws, policies, trends, and sentiments around what countries—and people within those countries—should be doing to make the world a better place. Essentially, world culture is the institutional isomorphism that occurs when the world polity and world society engage with nation-states to determine the future of progress. In other words, because of a centrally planned style of cultural globalization on the symbolic and institutional level, the ethos of countries begins to look rather similar.

That such a world culture exists is no longer a subject of much debate among global sociologists. Some of the more robust examples that demonstrate these cultural norm diffusions appear within education, human rights, environmentalism, and of course, technology adaptation. When nation-states change over time in their approach to these categories, the more involved they are with IGOs and INGOs, the more likely they are to change in the direction of world culture. Thus nations tied to IGO networks adopt laws and policies that are aligned with world cultural values such as mandatory secondary school enrollment for all, constitutional gender equality, environmental protectionism, and ICT use. Simultaneously, people within nations tied to INGO networks adopt these global values as well. Such a transference of values across contexts is often framed as a process of international norm diffusion.

Through this process, countries become more cosmopolitan and pass, for example, more environmentally conscious laws. Environmentalism is a world polity script developed over decades of conferences, including the Earth Summits in 1992 and 2002, the 2009 UN Climate Change Conference, as well as high profile treaties such as the 2016 Paris Agreement. Although the merits of such laws for environmental protection are self-evident, scholars do caution that there is a clear decoupling between laws and practice in many countries. One must only drive in the streets of Kathmandu once (or even take a brief ride as a passenger) to quickly learn that in many Global South countries laws are sometimes more like loose guidelines. The more elite one's status, the looser the guidelines are. Perhaps the greater issue with decoupling, however, is that the relative degrees of such policy-practice disconnects are clearly segregated along national income levels. As is true, in fact, for relative levels of nations' influential ties to the world polity/society.[46]

Simply stated, the poorer a country is, the lesser its ties to the world polity, and the higher the likelihood of decoupling between policy enactment and practical change.[47] Why would that be the case? Some scholars are convinced it is because the poorest countries in the world are forcefully caught up in *development* to their own detriment.[48] In the current models of globalization, to be using "developing" as a verb, the poorest nations in the world are required to grow their economy. In fact, many scholars use the term "development" as synonymous with gross domestic product (GDP) growth. Most traditional economists, in particular, measure a nation's "progress" simply as a function of GDP growth over time. To develop in this sense, poor countries must enter the global market for trade and economic exchange, and the contemporary global market is neoliberal to its core. In the global neoliberal markets, poor countries tend to face structural adjustment, austerity, and multinational corporate penetration in exchange for providing cheap labor and resources.[49] Beyond that, though, they also provide lands for outsourcing factory production and drilling, bodies of water for chemical pollution, and dumping grounds for electronic waste.

Laws, as a reminder, are oftentimes loose guidelines. The more powerful a global corporation, the looser the guidelines.

Unsurprisingly, then, regardless of how many Paris Agreements Global South countries sign, their capacity to enact meaningful environmental change is often thwarted by neoliberalism. It really comes down to this existential crisis faced by modern capitalism: if not the poorest Global South countries, *then where?* How can the production engines continue to create unfettered growth and unlimited wealth without the factories, the chemicals, and children laboring for a dime an hour? From a neoliberal economic standpoint, there is no alternative. But can't peripheral nations embody world cultural values of environmentalism *and* maintain the pressures of neoliberal economic development? Longhofer and Jorgenson, in a study of carbon emissions and economic development from 1970 to 2009, found that the answer is mostly *no.* In their study, economic development (read GDP growth) was associated with *more* carbon emissions in the poorest countries.[50] They found that economic development does contribute toward a slight decrease in emissions toward countries that have stronger ties to world society, however. These are relatively more developed countries that are the most plugged into global civil society networks. One must only spend a few hours in Kathmandu city to experience the dense cloud of smog concentrated with $CO_2$ and various poisonous gases that local residents are forced to accept as legitimate, breathable air.

World cultural values have the potential to enact some meaningful change, but such change is not equally accessible to the poorest countries that are dominated by global neoliberalism. What we can glean from the environmentalism example is that development can, in fact, be a hurdle in accomplishing progressive world cultural values. Since carbon emissions, for example, are a global problem, this leaves global civil society efforts at environmentalism as merely symbolic in a most generous interpretation. A more critical interpretation would suggest that middle- and higher-income nations are embedded within IGO and INGO networks to performatively signal global progress while also creating a world culture that pushes for neoliberal standards for "development." These very standards in effect render progress unattainable for the poorest countries, and therefore for the world as a whole. Crucially, of course, the notion of "development" itself is a world cultural script.[51]

## OTHER FACES OF "DEVELOPMENT"

What else is development? So far we have (1) another word for GDP growth and (2) a world cultural script for human progress. Some scholars suggest a third and substantially less becoming interpretation of development: a civilizing mission rebranded to discursively—if not quite practically—divorce itself from colonial legacy. In *Development Discourse and Global History: From Colonialism to the Sustainable Development Goals*, the postdevelopment scholar Aram Ziai provides an insightful perspective on development: "knowledge about *development* is the knowledge about the falsehood of others' way of living and their necessary correction."[52] In other words, development entails accepting the premise that some countries need to change in a very specific way so as to resemble other, "better" countries. For this change to materialize, the better, *developed* nations must guide, aid, and supervise the *underdeveloped* nations. This is a premise ingrained in development discourse and consequently accepted by development agencies, workers, and researchers. So we accept that some countries are better than others, that's just objective or scientific or whatever Western enlightenment term we are in the mood to use to justify making these hierarchical distinctions. But how exactly is this different from imperialism?

Colonized nations under imperialism were considered to be incapable of governing themselves. Such infantilization of peripheral nations is not only omitted but problematized within the new cosmopolitan mission of development. No, Western countries don't need to govern the Global South anymore, that's colonialism! They only need to serve as role models, as well as to occasionally provide aid to support the process of shaping the underdeveloped countries in their own image. The Global South will govern themselves into a state of postindustrial bliss if they just follow the path laid out by modern Western nations. Such is the premise of the ever-resilient modernization theory, which at a closer look will quickly reveal its do-it-yourself brand of neo-imperialism.[53]

The modernization model of development persists under neoliberal globalization in spite of the imperialist premise and the historical evidence of its many flaws. This premise of modernization goes as follows: by entering the global neoliberal "free markets," countries in the Global South could have access to unlimited economic growth and wealth. These countries would enter their resources and labor force into a global arena of free exchange, where in return they would be able to acquire capital. With this capital, they would be able to grow their GDP, build infrastructure, and *modernize*. This model pushed for industrialization and urbanization as key methods of attaining *modern* and *desirable* states: countries that mimicked powerful Western nations.[54] The process had worked for these rich nations, so it had to also work for poor nations!

It's easy to trace the imperial legacy of the modernization premise. European countries and their cousin the United States underwent a great industrial revolution, utilized their white wit and natural resources to create a ton of wealth and new technologies, and built fabulous modern civilizations with tall buildings and minimal poverty. Other, nonwhite countries, however, seemed to be stuck in their annoying habits of harboring absolute poverty. European leaders first met at the League of Nations and wondered what could be done about these other countries. They lamented over their white burdens, which were increasingly difficult to nurse under the new internationalism rhetoric the league itself was building. Colonization was just not trendy anymore. There had to be another way. Soon they realized that these other countries also had natural resources that could be exploited for growing modern civilizations. What the countries lacked, of course, was the white wit, which the better nations could supply in endless council at international IGO meetings. This is how, as Ziai states, "colonial discourse turned into the discourse of development."[55]

A slight problem, of course, is that things haven't quite turned out the way modernization theory predicted, with a handful of notable exceptions.[56] Both proponents of this paradigm and believers in the premise of development might suggest that things simply haven't turned out that way *yet*. There are scholars and policy makers who genuinely believe to this day that with enough industrialization and development projects *we will get there*. Sure, the 2015 deadline with the MDGs turned out to be unrealistic, but in 2030 we will meet the SDGs and finally, at long last, there will be no more hunger in this world, per goal number 1. As I write this in the middle of witnessing a historic global pandemic and economic collapse, I suspect we will fall slightly short of meeting the 2030 deadline as well. And no, it's not because of the pandemic, although that provides a nice scapegoat for the umpteenth failure of "development."

The real reason the SDGs, like its predecessor, are a symbolic farce destined to failure is that development follows the modernization premise, and modernization, plainly stated, is a lie. World-systems analysis understands the world as a single unit of capitalist operations, and Western nations would neither be able to attain modernization, nor maintain their wealth and power, without brutally and systematically exploiting the Global South. Only by extracting cheap labor and resources from periphery countries could the global core achieve such high concentrations of wealth. The neoliberal free market greatly aided this process. When it became far more profitable to outsource factories while charting local decreases in carbon emissions, the United States and other Western countries were entirely too eager to take their production and polluting activities to the Global South. Then climate change would also become the third world's fault! It was a win-win for the West because, as it turned out, Western multinational corporations (MNCs) didn't really have to pay local taxes or minimum wages in those countries. They could go even further and exercise new levels of power over those governments and dissuade them from providing welfare policies. They could destroy local businesses in seconds: which local beverage shop could compete with the resources of Coca-Cola? Periphery nations would be forced to accept these MNCs and their outrageous conditions because they needed to grow their GDPs and undergo development. Without the low-wage factory jobs, it was hard to grow the economy in these primarily agrarian nations. Subsistence agriculture did not command the kind of economic growth that "development" demanded. Neoliberalism provided Western nations via MNCs with access to previously unimaginable concentrations of wealth and power. The premise of development aided neoliberalism in reaching these heights.

For modernization theory to have legitimacy, the Global South would need to be able to extract cheap labor and resources from . . . where? The Earth, it turns out, would run out of poor countries to exploit eventually. Not to mention the air quality in Kathmandu, devastating floods in rural Nepal and Bangladesh, hurricanes, forest fires, and myriad climate catastrophes that have ensued from excessive industrialization. The Earth, as it turns out, would also run out of resources and stamina to deal with neoliberal capitalism. The brunt of these catastrophes are faced by the "developing" Global South, as the "developed" Global North reaps the brunt of the luxurious benefits.

Now enter ICTs and the attention economy. Powerful core nations can exploit the very humanity of Global South populations as the capitalist world-system responds to the threat of globally waning material resources. ICT4D tacitly cosigns this premise, just as prior development efforts have cosigned other forms of Global South abuse. Same old exploitation, new technology. How can "development" *not* be considered a form of neo-imperialism? Yet global civil society networks are really set on making development and ICT4D happen. Development is a world cultural script, and it must be appropriately diffused. The SDGs must go on. But if development programs don't really benefit developing populations, why do countries collude with these IGOs and INGOs to support development programs?

A country as a unit of analysis is extremely deceptive from the standpoint of power. It is fully accurate to state that some countries have power over other countries, but power operates on multiple simultaneous levels of society. What is often ignored in conversations about world culture and development is the notion of power *within* countries. Who holds power in any country? What about Global South countries, who holds power there? The ruling classes and elites tend to hold power in most capitalist societies, and radical systemic change tends to be against their direct material interests. In the Global South particularly, though, the ruling classes *share* power with another group with a benevolent reputation: INGOs.

The diffusers of world cultural norms amid local citizenry, INGOs, are not all created equal. In *The Authority Trap: Strategic Choices of International NGOs*, Sarah Stroup and Wendy Wong distinguish between "leading INGOs" and "other INGOs" based on their relative access to power. Other INGOs are smaller, less powerful organizations that tend to support radical change and make up the large majority of INGOs; whereas leading INGOs are a handful of extremely powerful organizations such as Amnesty International and Greenpeace that operate in the Global South to promote predominantly reformist agendas.[57] The way leading INGOs gain authority and power is by working with elite donors both in local and global contexts. Because their authority is tied into their connections with private donors and government networks, they have little latitude in promoting radical change. Thus they end up promoting tepid reforms that support the status quo. The other INGOs, who promote radical change, lack the power and authority they need for such change to materialize.

Civil society development programs are neoliberal imperialism. Powerful countries and powerful people within countries come together at world polity junctions to determine roadmaps for global progress. These road maps are always nonthreatening to their power and status quo. They are also often only symbolic and are rarely successful in achieving the stated reformist aims (for example, MDGs). World culture—i.e., cultural globalization—serves to symbolically manage the public relations optics for neoliberalism—i.e., economic globalization. Cultural globalization is the General Assembly to economic globalization's Security Council. The former is engaged in performative progressivism not only to dilute the latter's destructive neo-imperialist influence on the Global South but to actually *promote* neoliberal agendas vis-à-vis "development." All the while, masses of the people continue to struggle for access to food, clean water, and breathable air as national elites form power coalitions with civil society networks and dictate what it is that the people really need.

ICT4D as a world cultural script fits perfectly into such agendas as these programs promise to provide empowerment while allowing big tech firms and core countries to colonize the minds and hearts of Global South populations. If development is a form of imperialism, then ICT4D innovates imperialism to colonize bodies and minds without needing to colonize lands and spaces to the same extent. Through the world attention economic system, Global South people are exploited and mined; their hopes, dreams, and fears turned into capital—all while maintaining the premise of helping and empowering them.

# 3

# CASTE SOCIETY AND
# DEVELOPMENT BAIT

C ritiques of developmentalism have a rich history of scholarship within the world-systems, *dependency*, and *postdevelopment* traditions.[1] As discussed in chapter 2, development is an elite global script. As a member of the elite caste and class in Nepal, writing about these topics poses several challenges for me both intellectually and personally. The tendency among people like me to draw on our fortunate international education of the highest caliber to study "them" is all too strong. My hope here is to avoid that kind of framing and to put more of a focus on studying "us." Because, by and large, *we* are the managers of development, at least in Nepal and in many Global South nations.[2] In the official capacity, *we* tend to handle issues of development—and all the cash that comes with it via foreign aid and otherwise—so the subjects of development don't have to do so.

Despite our powerful position in managing development, we are a curiously understudied population, and little is written about us from a critical framework in academic literature (perhaps much of this is because we are often also framing the academic literature). This is, of course, not without exception. In his 1997 book *In the Name of Development: A Reflection on Nepal*, the geographer Nanda Shrestha outlined how Nepali elites consumed the narrative of development so they could fulfill their desires to adopt the luxurious lifestyles offered by Western development agents and, of course, development aid.[3] In this book, Shrestha grappled with some of the same questions I address here, undergoing a (kind of) parallel journey of self-reflection. Although, to be clear, Shrestha's journey was far more remarkable, harrowing, and inspiring. He grew up in absolute poverty in the now tourism paradise of Pokhara, before it was touched by development and its pioneers. Some of the narratives he shares about his childhood include often going to school hungry for several days in a row and missing out on festivities related to the Nepali national holiday of *Dashain* because his family was too poor to afford meat.

In this chapter, I build on Shrestha's arguments using cross-national data on information and communications technologies (ICTs) and international nongovernmental organizations (INGOs) to demonstrate that development initiatives historically and today serve elite populations in Global South countries while harming rural and Indigenous populations. Using the case example of Nepal, I demonstrate how existing structural tensions within Global South populations—in the case of Nepal, caste-based oppression—is exacerbated by development efforts. This perpetuates a cycle of unequal exchange in which development agents enrich already empowered populations but harm disempowered populations by exploiting land and resources. Such unequal exchange has been characteristic of development programs, and scholars have demonstrated the adverse impacts of development projects on health and environmental outcomes in the Global South. With information and communications technology for development (ICT4D), development agents carry the seeds of a specific kind of unequal exchange: exploiting attention and perpetuating the world attention economic system.

Beyond the theoretical and ethical implications of supporting such exploitative technology, ICT4D efforts also reinforce existing systems of unequal exchange by negating and minimizing rural populations. Development paradigms treat rural populations as bait: language around development often emphasizes rural empowerment, but in practice the vulnerabilities of rural Global South populations are used to successfully market development initiatives. Neoliberal at their core, ICT4D projects often *struggle to meet their own stated goals, such as expanding internet access.*

For instance, let's look at the World Summit on the Information Systems (WSIS) conventions in Geneva in 2003. At the convention, the idea of "ICT4D" was initially mainstreamed across the arena of development. This is one of the first instances when ICT4D was enshrined as world cultural script. After this convention, mobile phone services expanded globally and cell phone sales skyrocketed because they were now deemed crucial for global progress. The telecommunications industry experienced the largest boom in history, but rural populations in Nepal and other countries were still struggling to hop on the ICT train because basic telecommunications infrastructure never made it to some of these places. In theory, if development worked, prior iterations of such efforts should have already taken care of this issue; however, rural areas continue to struggle to overcome these basic hurdles.

In the world of neoliberal development, the rural is deliberately ignored except when it serves to emphasize the rhetoric of need in development spaces to promote more neoliberal capitalism. Although the entire resolution of the WSIS Geneva convention strived to invoke rural Global South populations, Article 13 in particular states that "*we are resolute* to empower the poor, particularly those living in remote, rural and marginalized urban areas, to access information and to use ICTs as a tool to support their efforts to lift themselves out of poverty."[4]

At the time of this writing, it has been nearly two decades since this resolution was made, and trillions of dollars have been earned in profits by telecommunications corporations. Yet rural areas in many parts of the Global South still lack access to reliable internet. Ignoring the "pull yourself up by your cell phone app" premise of the resolution, suggesting that poverty is the result of individual efforts (or lack thereof), the digital empowerment narrative of this of development initiative falls flat when faced with the empirical reality of uneven access to the internet in Global South countries.

## LEAVING THE RURAL BEHIND

Outside the elite metropolitan city of Kathmandu, Nepali people are struggling in ways that most people in the West would struggle to conceptualize. Rural Nepal consists of hundreds of Indigenous ethnicities occupying different regions, such as the Tharus living in the fertile agricultural regions and the Gurungs living along the basin of the Annapurna mountain range. The ruling classes (in Nepal, almost interchangeable with ruling *caste*), including the *brahmins and chettris*, mostly reside in the capital city and other hill regions, and rural Nepal is inhabited by folks either at the bottom of the caste hierarchy or those excluded by the caste system. The whole idea of development supposedly exists to uplift these specific populations—but rural Nepal is the epitome of development's ultimate failure.

Before "development" first began to take hold of my country, the majority of people in rural areas relied on subsistence farming. Although far from desirable living within a feudal or pseudo-feudal system, some scholars argue that most Nepali families had the ability to sustain their family's most basic needs then, including access to food and nutrition.[5] Shrestha specifically argues that before Western forces of development interfered, Nepali ethnicities across the country contained Indigenous knowledge passed on for generations that allowed them to farm productively while working with—and not against—nature. When he was growing up, Shrestha's hometown, Pokhara, was a village where most people grew their own food on small plots of land, revered *prakriti* (nature), and worked with Indigenous knowledge to sustain the village. As Shrestha write, "the indigenous economic systems and values were generally self-reliant, self-sufficient, sustainable and far less destructive to both humanity and nature. It served as a hedge against total depravation. But now under the banner of development, the dignity and humanity of the poor were being questioned whereas poverty itself appeared to be deepening."[6]

Today Pokhara is a large metropolitan city that serves as a tourist paradise and produces large amounts of pollutants to sustain the lifestyle of foreign tourists, and Indigenous farming techniques are all but eradicated from its economy.[7]

Pokhara was gentrified in Shrestha's lifetime by development agents. Due to relatively easy access from Kathmandu and desirable landscapes as a valley engulfed by prominent mountain ranges on all sides, Pokhara underwent the process of modernization and its native residents were forced to give up their lands and livelihoods to make way for development and "progress." Most other villages across Nepal, where a large majority of the population resides (79 percent as of 2020[8]), would require massive investment in roads and transportation infrastructure to be made accessible for gentrification. Completing such infrastructure projects would require investing more international aid on the actual projects than on the bank accounts of elite development workers, so the process has been staggeringly slow.

Nepal is divided into three broad topographical categories, the agrarian plains (Terai) at the bottom, the hill districts in the middle, and the mountain districts (Himalayas) at the top.

Today, many decades later, it is possible to travel by road to most of the fertile Terai regions of Nepal; however, there is no reliable way to reach the most destitute parts of the country—the world famous Himalayas. The topography of the mountains make them a poor infrastructural investment in transportation. The costs would be high and the benefits minimal. Some high-profile mountain ranges, such as Everest, have enough infrastructure to support tourism, but the requirements are minimal because the adventure tourists come to Nepal for trekking and don't need high quality driving roads.

After the introduction of development and tourism, in the more high-profile districts such as Solukhumbu (home to Mount Everest), Indigenous populations such as Sherpa communities have been forced to make a livelihood supporting the tourists in their climbing hobbies. The less globally desirable rural mountains of Humla and Jumla are completely forgotten in the process of development. So are the more destitute hill regions of Rukum and Rolpa. By the 1990s, when development became the status quo for the Nepalese economy, some of the poorest members of oppressed castes in Nepal resided in Rukum and Rolpa. These parts of the country were left to such destitution that their populations started a guerrilla armed revolution that ended with the removal of King Gyanendra Bir Bikram Shah and the end of absolute monarchy in Nepal in 2006.

## ICT FOR DEVELOPMENT
## AND RURAL ACCESS

I describe the Nepali Civil War in depth in subsequent chapters, especially the second interlude, but here I want to highlight how development has correlated with rural erasure from the beginning. After the Washington consensus of the 1980s, development began to fuse so fully with neoliberal agendas that development remains inseparable from liberalization today. INGOs target rural development, but they operate within a neoliberal economic status quo in which the rural does not even really have the right to exist. In my own research I have evaluated these contradictions, as have many scholars before me.

The erasure of rural populations is apparent in the case of ICTs for development (ICT4D). Although ICT4D programs tend to emphasize rural areas, these areas in the most economically dependent Global South countries still lag in access. In a study looking across 133 Global South countries from 1995 to 2014, my coauthor Sam Shirazi and I found that the intersections of economic dependency and rurality are crucial to understanding cross-national inequalities in ICT access.[9] World systems scholars have consistently demonstrated the negative impact of liberalization and neoliberal policies on several development outcomes, including environmental degradation and health. Our study found that high levels of neoliberal policies, such as expanded export concentration and foreign investment, corresponded to lower levels of access to mobile phones in the Global South. Economic insecurity faced by developing nations relying on volatile markets to export small number of commodities negatively impacted national mobile phone access. As with other forms of inequality, digital inequality is also reproduced through unequal trade practices that disadvantage developing nations in neoliberal global markets. Crucially, the disadvantage is *exacerbated* in nations that have larger rural populations.

Below I share results from an expansion on the previous study, including four additional time points leading up to the year 2018 that are now available for analysis. As figure 3.1 shows, adding these more recent years to the analysis reinforces the patterns previously identified. This updated analysis shows how economic dependency and levels of rurality continue to intersect to exclude the poorest rural populations from ICT access across 133 Global South countries from 1990 to 2018.

Figure 3.1 shows that digital inequality stems from disproportionate rural exclusion in economically dependent lower-income countries. The poorest countries who are most dependent on other nations for aid and resources and have the highest rural populations face the highest levels of digital inequality. The premise of modernization is that more neoliberalism leads to more "development" (a term used almost synonymously with "industrialization"), which invokes sharply urban characteristics. Rural areas are simply theoretical urban spaces of the future. The needs of the rural population ultimately don't matter from a development standpoint because, after sufficient levels of

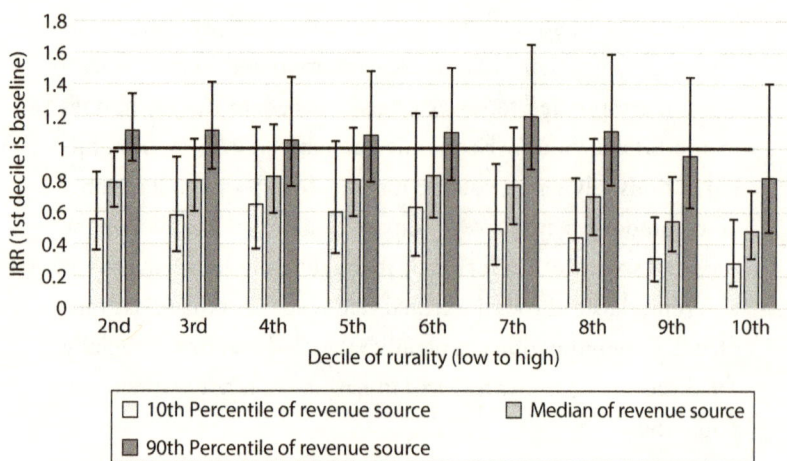

FIGURE 3.1 Incident rate ratios of mobile phone subscriptions by decile of rurality and level of revenue, 1990 to 2018.

neoliberal intervention have been enacted, there will be no more rural areas left in the world.

Rural areas are perpetually excluded even though "development" discourse uses the plight of rural populations to promote their agendas. In addition to weakening a developing state's economic capacity, neoliberal globalization is designed to ignore rural populations in Global South countries entirely. This process is apparent in the case of ICTs. The negative effects of increased fiscal dependence on mobile phone access are more pronounced after accounting for differences in rural populations between countries, suggesting that rurality and dependency are closely interlinked in how they influence digital inequality.

This makes sense considering the severe lack of investment in the massive telecommunications infrastructure required to successfully operate ICTs in rural areas. Especially in the poorest most dependent countries, development elites are unwilling to invest in rural infrastructure. Development elites are not going to be living in rural areas, so ultimately they don't care. As long as they serve as the intermediaries accepting and building wealth off development aid under the guise of supporting rural areas, their interests are met. There is no real need to actually provide any services to rural populations because under a modernization premise they only exist in a perpetually temporary state of being.

It is interesting that richer Global South countries (i.e., countries that have higher fiscal independence) *can* effectively neutralize the negative effects of high rurality. These countries also categorically have smaller percentages of their populations residing in rural areas and have more disposable income to invest in telecommunications infrastructure more evenly across the national geography. Thus Global South countries with high urban populations do not appear to be as affected by digital inequality across levels of fiscal independence. In other words, high dependency *and* high rurality create the most precarious conditions for nations to become subjected to increased digital inequality.

Nepal falls into the category of a country with high rural populations and low fiscal independence. Nepal has consistently failed to build necessary infrastructure even in the urban capital, so it has limited capacity—or will—to expand telecommunications infrastructure in rural areas.

## INGOs CANNOT SAVE DEVELOPMENT

Explicit developmentalism via INGO expansion does little to exacerbate digital inequality affecting the rural Global South. Figure 3.2 shows that, with very high levels of INGO

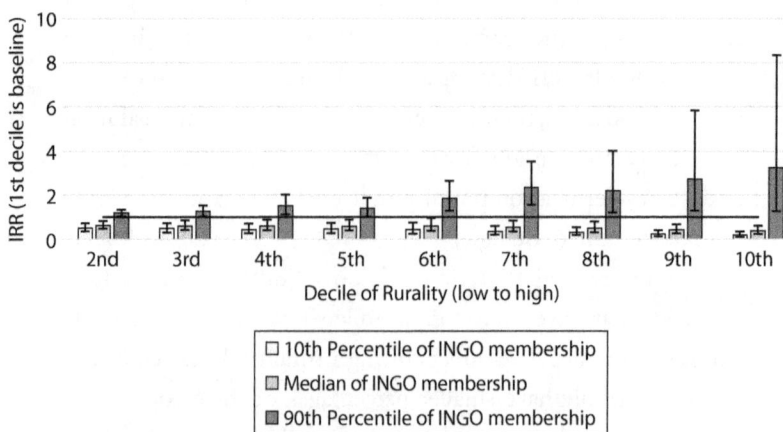

FIGURE 3.2 Incident rate ratios of mobile phone subscriptions by decile of rurality and level of INGO membership, 1990 to 2018.

membership, the negative effect of rurality on mobile phone access can perhaps be somewhat mitigated. Across 133 countries, those with high rural populations and an exceptionally high concentration of INGOs experience less digital inequality.

In practice, there are two issues. First, the high concentration of INGOs needed to neutralize the effects of rurality do not exist in the lowest income countries. As figure 3.3 shows, upper-middle-income countries consistently had the highest concentration of INGOs compared to lower-middle- and lower-income countries from 1995 to 2018. Second, the limited number of INGOs that operate in the lowest income nations have been known to populate around relatively affluent, suburban regions. In Nepal, for example, even though there are hundreds of INGOs, most of them are based in the capital city of Kathmandu or very close to the capital city, where the ruling caste elites reside.[10]

When considering who manages development, this is not all that surprising. Elites in Nepal want modernism and luxury, affluences that are not available in rural areas that lack the most

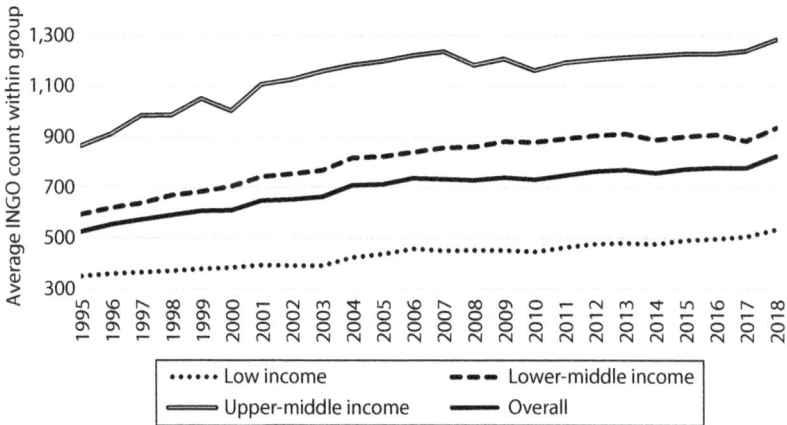

FIGURE 3.3 Average INGO count by state group and year from 1995 to 2018.

basic infrastructure such as running water. To put it simply, members of the ruling elite that manage development and foreign aid do not want to live in rural Nepal because they are savvy enough to know that these places are neither developed, nor "developing," in any meaningful way. For these areas to be "developing," the same people who work in the development sector to expand their wealth would have to sincerely invest in rural areas from building infrastructure to providing access to basic resources such as food and clean water. These areas are too undesirable for the development elite to live in, and improving the standard of living in these areas is not their genuine concern. That is not why they work in the development sector. Elites in Nepal do not have to care for the oppressed castes and economically vulnerable people residing in these areas because their caste status provides them with the spiritual authority to exclude and ignore rural populations.

## CASTE IN NEPAL

Development efforts homogenize Global South countries, even though every country deals with unique forms of inequality within their national and cultural borders. These inequalities affect the development process: in many cases, ruling elites within a country benefit at the cost of the subjugated. In Nepal, the caste system produces the dehumanization that elites adopt at the individual level because for centuries our society has upheld a belief system that assigns divine will to brutal and most exploitative segregation.[11]

Caste is a system of stratification in South Asian Hindu societies that hierarchically divide people based on religious attributes. The technicalities of the system alone could fill up many books, but broadly the caste system is divided into four major occupational categories known as "varnas": brahmins/bauns (priests), chettris (warriors), vaishyas (traders), and shudras (laborers). People that fall into one of these categories are savarnas (i.e., with caste) and those who fall outside of these categories such as Indigenous populations or non-Hindus are classified as avarna (i.e., without caste). The classifications in Nepal are a little bit different, with hundreds of Indigenous groups represented within its small borders. Nepal is ethnically heterogenous with 125 different ethnic groups separated at the intersection of geography and caste position.[12] Nonetheless, the broad categorizations suffice to understand the community I come from. Brahmins, or *baun* in Nepali, the priestly caste, are at the top of the hierarchy and considered closest to God. Hindu scripture indicates that one arrives at this highest status after reincarnating many times over as people of lower status and proving their worth with each rebirth.[13] Thus Hindu society subscribes to the idea that caste divisions are "based not on birth but (worth)."[14]

Caste status, of course, also corresponds to social, political, and economic power. Savarnas, particularly *bauns*, chettris and vaishyas, control the socioeconomic, cultural, and political landscape of Hindu societies. Bhimrao Ramji Ambedkar's *Castes in India: Their Mechanism, Genesis, and Development* provides a thorough explanation for how their classifications came to be through a process of iterative rules for endogamy.[15] The rules include widow self-immolation and child marriage for young girls. In general, people in dominant caste groups are religiously educated to not only believe that they have spiritually *earned* their superior status in society but that it is their job to govern over those lower on the hierarchy as a method of helping them move up the hierarchy in future incarnations. Here we have already arrived at a sociocultural context in which the ruling elite derives spiritual meaning from the subjugation of certain subaltern groups. Yet we have only scratched the surface on the depths to which caste societies produce systematic subjugation and dehumanization.

The shudras provide their (often very cheap) labor to the dominant castes for a chance at a better life in future births, and the avarna folks get the status of a pollutant, historically known as *Dalit* and, interchangeably, "untouchable." Growing up in a traditional *baun* household, I distinctly remember elders and grandparents refusing to eat certain meals because they had been cooked by "an untouchable," or a person deemed as such was simply present in the kitchen when the meal was being prepared. As a child it was mostly befuddling, given they tended to employ mostly avarna folks—specifically members of Indigenous *Tharu* ethnicity—as domestic help in my house. Looking back now, I recognize this wasn't merely a rude eccentricity my grandpa's sister enjoyed but was a discriminatory practice codified in the laws of Nepal, a country that was proudly "the only Hindu nation in the world" prior to the Nepali Civil War that ended in 2006.

Refusing meals cooked by folks without caste might sound relatively benign when we begin to consider the brutal human rights abuses committed against oppressed caste communities that continue to take place in Hindu societies today. Take, for example, the case of twenty-one-year-old Nabaraj B. K., a young Dalit man whose dead body was discovered on the banks of the Bheri River in rural Nepal in June 2020.[16] Three of his Dalit friends were also found dead in the river. A mob of villagers violently murdered the four young men because Nabaraj's "crime" was that he fell in love with a dominant-caste woman. His friends faced the mob judiciary for conspiring to help the couple elope. In one of innumerable cases over many decades, an entire village was ready to commit brutal violence to protect the supposed purity of the Hindu caste system.

When one accepts the premise that those at the bottom of the hierarchy not only deserve but actually *need* violent exploitation for their own spiritual development, one completely loses the ability to feel any remorse. When a society accepts the same premise, human lives are treated as completely disposable in favor of "greater spiritual pursuits." The oppressed die, and the dominant celebrate their own position in the hierarchy and congratulate themselves for their moral and spiritual superiority. It's all in the Hindu scripture. It was codified into Nepali law as well until recently. As Ambedkar writes in *Annhilation of Caste*, his powerful manifesto against the caste system: "Caste may be bad. Caste may lead to conduct so gross as to be called man's inhumanity to man. All the same, it must be recognized that the Hindus observe Caste not because they are inhuman or wrongheaded. They observe Caste because they are deeply religious."[17]

## CASTE AND THE INTELLECTUAL PREMISE OF DEVELOPMENT

It is under these cultural contexts that the ruling elite of Nepal, who are also members of the dominant castes and of the intellectual class, promote their ideas of "development." Although ideas about development were brought into the mold by colonizers and foreign imperialists, at least in the case of Nepal, the colonizers built their house on the solid, preexisting foundation of a deeply violent historical system of stratification. Once the elites adopted the rhetoric of development, it became the dominant paradigm for progress. Who was going to argue with the ruling elite? Ambedkar writes: "in every country the intellectual class is the most influential class, if not the governing class. The intellectual class is the class which can foresee, it is the class which can advise and give the lead. In no country does the mass of the people live the life of intelligent thought and action. It is largely imitative, and follows the intellectual class."[18]

In Nepal and many Hindu societies, the intellectual class highly correlates with dominant castes and with economic class. Historically speaking, intellectual pursuits were analogous to religious pursuits, so the priest was the scholar.[19] Religious knowledge was the key knowledge people sought, so priests possessed all the knowledge that was deemed socially worthy. This left a legacy of brahmins taking on the role of the intellectual long before Western enlightenment secularized education. For example, my own grandfather was a renowned scholar of history who wrote many influential books and received several honors from the monarchy for his intellectual contributions. In his youth, he simply worked as a *baun* priest. My own positionality as a brahmin-born intellectual is also not lost on me as I write this book.

As Ambedkar states, the intellectual class determines the social and cultural standards for conduct and progress, in addition to governing communities in countries like Nepal. Thus, when the intellectual class adopts the framework of development, it quickly becomes the dominant paradigm for national progress. Nanda Shrestha elaborates on the role of these elite forces in mainstreaming development throughout his book: "The whole process of development, both in theory and praxis, is little more than ruling elites' concentrated efforts to replicate the West by decorating the national economic and sociocultural landscapes with material glory, the ultimate symbol of Western modernity."[20]

Here two themes simultaneously emerge. First is the idea that development in Nepal is a concentrated effort from the ruling elite, i.e., development is a ruling class project by dominant caste communities. Second, the ruling class in Nepal undertakes such a project hoping to emulate Western material standards of progress. These standards, of course, were brought in through colonial forces. Although never "officially" colonized, Nepal remained the de facto subcolony of British India throughout much of the colonial period (1858–1947).[21]

To attain the kinds of material success that would enable Nepali elites to live modern Western lives, they needed to rapidly increase their wealth in the immediate postcolonial period. The best way for Global South elites to access that kind of wealth was by securing a piece of the foreign aid pie that came along when they accepted the project of "development."[22] Throughout the second part of the twentieth century, development often meant accepting foreign aid to increase industrial production and (theoretically) expand infrastructure. By participating in development, the rich could become incredibly richer, but the poorer and rural populations watched their natural environments destroyed and their sustainable agricultural lifestyle become threatened by modernity.

The fact of the matter is, at least in Nepal, development aid rarely worked as intended. Consider infrastructure alone. In the late 1990s to the early 2010s, Nepal received tens of millions (U.S. dollars) in loans and aid from the Asian Development Bank and other organizations for specific development projects designed to expand hydroelectricity across the country using our abundant freshwater resources. When I was growing up, I regularly heard about the famous Melamchi Water Supply Project, which was supposed to provide bountiful access to clean water and electricity in Kathmandu, where these resources were scarce.[23] Occasionally I would hear that they received more funding for this project, and I would get excited only to realize that my dreams for clean water and uninterrupted electricity were not going to be realized.

By the time I left Nepal at the age of eighteen to travel to the United States for college, I had spent the better part of the preceding decade without regular access to electricity. "Load-shedding," was the term used to describe why the government shut down the power in different areas across Kathmandu valley for several hours each day.[24] In my last two or three years living in Nepal, our house was sometimes on a 4/20 load-shedding schedule. That is, during the dry winter months, sometimes we only got four hours a day of electricity. Those of us with privilege worked around this somewhat by installing micro generators in our homes that gave us an additional five or six hours of electricity a day (depending on which appliances you ran in addition to the fridge; my desktop computer was a point of contention with my whole family because the selfish teenager I was did not shy away from using up a lot of this limited power to go online). In those days, I would often wonder *whatever happened to the Melamchi project? Weren't they the ones supposed to save me and give me more internet time?*

Not being able to access the internet whenever I wanted to was pretty much all I was concerned with at the time, but looking back now those years were *tough*. To this day, there are still moments when I freeze in the realization that all the things I take for granted—clean water, electricity, and unlimited internet—simply were not accessible to me for the first decades of my life. Such was my experience as a *baun, upper-class, Kathmandu elite*. When I was growing up, development didn't even serve *me* the way it was supposed to (although it surely benefited me and my elite community in other ways), so what reason would I ever have to expect that it would serve poor people in remote and rural areas of Nepal? As Shrestha writes: "There is evidence to suggest that development—whether internally induced or externally generated—does increase national wealth. But poverty is rarely abated as it continues to sharpen its teeth against the poor, right in the midst of growing wealth. Nepal typically exemplifies the cliché that the rich get richer and the poor poorer. Since 1950

Nepal's per capita income has more than doubled, but so has its incidence of poverty and destitution, a parallel trajectory that has become the historical landmark of capitalist development."[25]

Development has become the very process through which the most disadvantaged populations experience further depravation. This has been demonstrated by various schools of thought across the social sciences, including world-systems, dependency and postdevelopment theoretical traditions.[26] As development is pushed across the Global South, similar patterns emerge across other countries in Asia,[27] Latin America,[28] and sub-Saharan Africa,[29] showing that economic growth ("development") correlates with higher income inequality and elites reap the largest benefits. Many societies have preexisting systems of stratification that are ready to exacerbate at the onset of development. As a Hindu nation, Nepal was already segregated socially and economically. Development expanded these inequalities substantially, partially explaining the decade-long civil war that transpired around the turn of the millennium.

In Nepal, as inequality expands even today, elites continue to justify their luxury using the age-old Hindu rhetoric that gives them spiritual satisfaction. In their hearts and souls they feel that oppressed caste folks in rural areas are simply living out their divine destiny of suffering. They never think about how their attempts at development are actively expanding the suffering of the most destitute populations of Nepal. They rest assured that everyone is spiritually better off when they horde all the foreign aid and give nothing in return.

Foreign aid, without a doubt, is most materially beneficial to development sector elites in Global South countries like Nepal. Other major beneficiaries of aid are foreign development agents who set up shop in the Global South. In Nepal, for example, Shrestha writes: "It is no exaggeration that foreign aid is perhaps

the biggest welfare scam in the arena of international development, holding underdeveloped countries hostage while fattening
the already bulging coffers of various interest groups within the
development establishment—both at the national and international levels."

I admire Shrestha's bold proclamation that "foreign aid" is a
*scam*. I may not go that far, but I am sympathetic to the framing. Empirical studies continue to show the benefits of foreign
aid to underdeveloped nations, but many of these studies are
missing the metaphorical forest for the metaphorical trees.[30]
Inequality within countries is the *outcome* of the imperialist status quo of the post–World War II development. Studies after
studies show economic growth—the most traditional goal of
"development"—is correlated with massive increases in inequality across geographic regions. Foreign development aid may
help some struggling communities under certain circumstances;
however, it *always* expands the wealth of people working in the
development sector in Global South countries. Often, the people
expanding wealth from these sectors are elite groups who have
social and intellectual capital. Their interests are aligned with
inequality on all fundamental levels: economic, social, political,
and especially in the case of Nepal, *religious*. To believe that these
communities will utilize foreign aid to simultaneously "solve"
inequality is paradoxical thinking.

## DEVELOPMENT 2.0
## AND NEOLIBERAL CAPITALISM

Crucially, aid is only one aspect of development, and since the
1980s neoliberalism has promoted a new form of development
known as structural adjustment.[31] We can take this concept
quite literally: structural adjustment is when global financial

institutions such as the IMF and the World Bank provide loans to adjust the economic structure of Global South nations. These conditional loans are provided to expand development and infrastructure in return for liberalizing the economies of poor nations.[32] In other words, this money is a bribe to elites to allow Global North countries to ravage the natural resources, ecosystems, and human potential of Global South countries until they are left facing the worst effects of global industrial production. From floods to landslides, droughts, and earthquakes, there is no shortage of expanding natural disasters in the developing world as a direct result of "development" under neoliberalism and policies such as structural adjustment.[33]

Without even considering the harsher environmental impacts—such as, for example, the historically devastating floods in the agricultural regions of Nepal in 2020[34]—that affect the poorest populations, there is the consideration of everyday pollution and standard of living. Everyone in Kathmandu, elites and otherwise, are required to breathe the same air. Aside from migration—which was how I escaped—even elites cannot figure out how to make the negative impacts of air pollution more unequal. The air quality in Kathmandu is so toxic it consistently ranks among the worst in the world, with the Air Quality Index (AQI) showing record high levels of 500 in 2021.[35]

It might be tempting to file away unbreathable air as some curious abnormality of Global South cities, but it's worth spending some time considering the everyday implications. Every time a person in Kathmandu goes out for a leisurely walk—an activity popular for its physical and mental health benefits—the person's physical health takes a toll because of the toxins, and mental health may also take a toll because of the dreary quality of the surroundings. Imagine agreeing to a science experiment requiring you to inject some harmful chemicals into your veins every time you leave your house. That dystopian experiment is the lived reality of all Kathmandu city dwellers the moment they leave their homes, and many Kathmandu residents are unhoused and are left bathing in the toxins on the streets of the city.

This is the result of industrialization and development, of opening up our economic borders to Global North corporations. While Nepali elites expanded their wealth in the process, they also signed away their own right to breathing clean air. In this tragicomedy of global political economy, Nepali elites are complicit in their own suffering in the process of actively magnifying the suffering of oppressed populations. The elites have traded the ability to buy luxury goods and travel across the world for a reality where the moment they return home they pay for these luxuries with their own health and sense of well-being. It is no wonder that there has been a massive increase in mental illness among elite populations in Nepal in recent years, but the mental health crisis is most prevalent among oppressed caste communities.[36] Nobody in the Global South is winning, but some are losing a lot more brutally than others.

Pervasive mental illness is characteristic across all types of populations in late capitalist society.[37] Even if ICT4D efforts did not often fail at their own stated goals of providing ICT access for all, they would run into a secondary problem of potentially worsening mental health outcomes in the Global South by exploiting rural populations to mine their data and reproduce the attention economy. The "service" they promote is misleading. As more people in rural communities in the Global South have smartphones and internet access, the ruling class in the attention economy acquires more workers. Rural populations do acquire some new utility functions—such as the ability to search for information and connect with loved ones—but the costs of access to these functions in the form of their personhoods are arguably unequal to the services received in their current iteration.

# INTERLUDE 2

## BEING EXTREMELY ONLINE AGAINST THE BACKDROP OF AN ARMED REVOLUTION

Even today I struggle to look back and clearly delineate what was truth and what was propaganda, or whose propaganda. Was it really unsafe to ride on the Safa Tempo (Nepali version of the Tuktuk)? Were tempos and microbuses so frequently bombed? The years blend in my mind, but these accounts of unpredictable bombings all around the city of Kathmandu definitely started to pop up in my early teenage years when I did rely on public transportation to independently get around. I can somewhat date the fear of bombs because these narratives were on the English-language daily newspapers I used to read to be current and hip with my global elite classmates in high school. I also remember regularly being upset that I wasn't allowed to go to social gatherings because public transportation was not safe. The other kids' parents had cars, many even had drivers. We had one motorcycle that was shared for all household needs, and dropping a fourteen-year-old girl at the movies (another place of frequent bombing . . . reports? rumors?) was not a priority.

So I stayed indoors a lot during my high school years, but I was totally fine with that because my computer was at home and it was so much more fun to talk to my online friends than be the awkward kid all the rich kids sneered at. My high school had a club called "The Aaru-busters" that was dedicated to making fun of me. Don't feel bad for me, I was kind of a jerk to be honest, but it was hardly my fault that I did not understand the social cues of the ludicrously rich world that I had joined in high school. Seriously, so rich I still can't wrap my mind around how rich they are in a country that is devastatingly poor. I was, of course, upper class by any normally distributed metric, but it never felt that way. As a teenager, I did not understand my relative privilege, which is so silly because extreme, grueling poverty was across my front door. I thought we were just fully poor!

In truth I never wanted to go anywhere or do anything because my limited pocket money would not cut it, and they would find out just how poor I was and that would be humiliating. My online friends from around the world literally did not know or care about my finances and class position. It was so much easier to socialize in this way, and it was free! Free to me, but my mom often complained about the large landline bills I ran up. The social component of my early internet use felt so empowering and in a way Web 2.0 is designed not to be.

At the time, what I appreciated the most was that I was living in a wholly different world as everything seemed to crumble outside my walls. The Nepali Civil War had begun in 1996 and encompassed much of my childhood in Nepal.[1] By 1996 militant civil strife was occurring outside Kathmandu in the rural centers of Rukum, Rolpa, and Gorkha. But it was not until much later, around 2001 or 2002, that the spoils of war first began to engulf the capital.[2] The war simply did not exist for me and my social strata. Occasionally I would hear adults deliberate at gatherings and parties about the threat of these *maobadi* (Maoists), with statements ranging from "they're just some rowdy youngsters, not a real threat" to "they are all terrorists who should be publicly beaten and murdered by the police."

As a child, I simply pictured the *maobadi* as one person in a big comic book villain outfit. The police, of course, were the superheroes in this narrative. I was particularly incentivized to internalize this heroic vision of the police from a young age. One of the families we always spent time with growing up was deeply connected to the Nepali federal law enforcement. My closest friends in my early life were the children of a man who went on to become inspector general in Nepal shortly before the revolution. Again, upon reflecting, it's impossible to know how much of my parents' affinity to that man—let's call him *Mukesh*—was earnest friendship, and how much of it was banking on a lifetime of favors. An example of one such favor was when my family drew on his influence to get me admitted to the extremely prestigious Rato Bangala School in nineth grade.

This was, and remains, virtually impossible to pull off. This K–12 institution is consistently recognized as one of the best schools in the world. Yes, *the world*. Admissions are open for first grade and A-Levels (eleventh grade equivalent), and it is difficult to get in at any other time. The school consistently sends its graduates to Ivy League colleges in the United States every year, partly because it recruits the smartest kids in the country at eleventh grade who go on to earn the highest global scores in Cambridge International A-Level exams. Almost nobody gets admitted at any other point, but I did. It was not because of my latent genius—I failed almost every class throughout my first year there. The details were minimally communicated to me, but I remember hearing that there were no open spots. That is, there were no spots until my mom made a phone call to Mukesh, and a few days later there was suddenly an open spot. In my micro-orbit, Nepal police earned their superhero stature.

Writing critically about these experiences is difficult because I must maintain intellectual objectivity and honor the integrity of the truths at play, while also navigating a very real sense of personal gratitude. Without attending Rato Bangala School, I would never have been able to move to the United States for college on a nearly full scholarship. I would not be in a position to share these narratives while reflecting upon broad historical patterns of reality. This book would never exist. It is with this caveat that I transition to unveiling the illusions of my young personhood.

What got me into the school was power. Some of that power accumulated by people like Mukesh went into navigating everyday obstacles, such as setting up—against stated odds—some *baun* girl to access more future power. I yield that very power in these pages today to ask: What was the cost of my own success?

In the early 2000s when I was attending this elite high school and traveling the world on my computer, children and teenagers my age across villages in Nepal were watching their family members publicly beaten to death and forced to take up arms against the Nepali state authority.[3] In his book *The Bullet and the Ballot Box*, the journalist Aditya Adhikara traces the scaling up of the Maoist insurgency to a specific event that transpired in November 1995.[4] The civil war began shortly after in 1996, when I was six years old. By 1995 the Maoists were mainly an ideological collective undertaking political education efforts in rural areas populated by impoverished masses of the oppressed castes. The underdeveloped villages in Rukum and Rolpa districts were the centers of operation for the early ideological activities of what eventually became the Communist Party of Nepal (Maoist) (CPN-M). The leaders of this movement, such as Baburam Bhattrai and Pushpa Kamal Dahal ("Prachanda"), were engaged in educating rural populations about the threats of authoritarianism and especially the monarchy. Through the early years of 1990, Maoist leaders occasionally found themselves in altercations with law enforcement and sometimes succeeded in securing arms and causing disruptions to local law enforcement and inciting mayhem at rural police stations.

These disruptions caught the attention of the Royal Nepali government, who responded with spectacularly visionary self-prophesying that sowed the seeds for their own destruction. In 1995, the government unleashed "Operation Romeo" on Rolpa, Dang, and Rukum districts.[5] The focus of the operation was to diffuse the militant Maoist uprising that was taking hold in those regions. The operation itself involved dispersing 2,200 armed police officers to villages across these districts to identify and neutralize suspected Maoist activists. What actually transpired was a widespread act of police violence and brutality that many human rights organizations nationally and internationally considered unprecedented.[6] The police indiscriminately raped, beat, and murdered people in numerous households, most of whom had no connection whatsoever with the insurgency.

For the insurgents, this tragedy served a purpose: oppressed communities across these districts witnessed and experienced firsthand the brutal aggression of the state. The Maoists declared a Civil War a few months later, much sooner than they had expected or planned to do. After suffering from the hands of law enforcement, experiencing unimaginable levels of violence, watching their family members get raped and murdered, the communities affected by Operation Romeo underwent a political awakening. The Maoists were not only able to recruit many new comrades but also were able to count on the political support of individuals and families that did not militantly engage in the war. State violence served as the very catalyst that accelerated the war and led to the eventual fall of the Nepali monarchy a decade later.

Not a single person I interacted with in that decade ever mentioned the tragedy. I suspect most people in my social orbit had no idea because their lives were completely consumed by pro-government, pro-police propaganda. Others in my orbit—such as my family's dear friend and my own savior Mukesh—were likely involved in the "project" in some capacity. If not directly involved in Operation Romeo, Mukesh certainly engaged and designed subsequent acts of police violence that continued to escalate as the insurgency grew after 1995. He did not become inspector general without appeasing the monarchy throughout the decade of war.

This figure, the possible architect of several large-scale human rights abuses, was to my family just a cool dude with a lot of power to do nice things for us.

Throughout the war our orbits stayed within the supervillain *maobadi* narrative. There was no alternative way of thinking. The newspapers said so, the television said so, everyone at the party said so. Even if an alternative was presented, even if my own family heard about the brutal violence these rural communities faced, I am going to have to be very honest and say that they would not care. Recall the brahmin fabric of my community, at the heart of which lies the fundamental belief that members of the oppressed castes exist in spiritual reality to experience suffering. Without experiencing suffering and serving the needs of the brahmins and chettris (such as the monarchy), these souls would have no chance of moving up the hierarchy in subsequent lifetimes until they attained the apotheosis of brahminhood. After all, even if they have no living memories of these experiences, they themselves went through the righteous passages of extreme suffering throughout many lifetimes to achieve their present brahminhood.

Operation Romeo and the decade of state violence that followed mostly affected the *kamaiyas* (day laborers) and *achuts* (untouchables). As far as dominant caste communities in Kathmandu were concerned, they were not actually human beings. It did not matter what the police and the monarchy did to them. What mattered was that Mukesh helped me get into Rato Bangala School. What mattered was that King Birendra honored my grandfather with an award for excellence in teaching, and the picture illustrating this remains proudly displayed in our family home in Kathmandu.

It was not until Birendra died in the June 2001 Nepali Royal Massacre that Kathmandu elites began to experience the sense of chaos that had been echoing throughout the country for years.[7] I remember that night more vividly than most other events from my childhood. I had been home from school sick with a very high fever. My mom had finally gotten me to sleep around midnight. An hour later the phone rang—the house phone that never rang after hours. Everyone heard the loud and obnoxious dinging. Landlines really added a dramatic effect to emergency situations. Something was obviously very wrong. My mom was making gestures of shock and horror like I had never heard or seen before. I was really scared. I wondered which one of my loved ones had died.

It was Mukesh calling to inform us that there had been a shooting at a dinner party at the Narayanhiti Royal Palace, and everyone in the royal family was dead. The first feeling I remembered was relief; all my loved ones were alive! Then came the shock and chaos. We started calling other families, and most had no clue. We gathered around the TV to watch the news. Nepal Television (NTV: the official government news channel and the only one that existed at the time) was offline. Five hours later a cousin informed us that BBC news was reporting on it.

The "report" was a two-minute segment stating that there was a massacre and that many members of the royal family were dead. We had gotten more detailed information than that in a private phone call that came hours after the incident. I say this only to emphasize the reach my family had.

Shockingly, this event—the massacre itself, at least—was unrelated to the civil war. Although questions remain unanswered and many conspiracy theories populate across Nepali communities even today, the official historical record indicates that the crown prince Dependra shot his whole family before shooting himself over a family dispute.[8] One of the most popular conspiracy theories at the time insisted that Birendra's brother, Gyanendra, who seceded him to the throne, orchestrated the massacre. Nobody fully knows what happened in that palace that night. All investigations were shut down within two weeks, and offers to conduct forensic testing from the international community were refused.

Regardless of what actually happened, the Nepali people, especially Kathmandu residents, despised Gyanendra and rejected him as king. The way people saw it, at the very least he was guilty of surviving the massacre along with his wife and son, when every other member of the royal family died that night. Birendra, it seemed, was adored by elite Nepali communities. The benevolent king, the one to instate constitutional monarchy, regal in his appearance, the human incarnation of Lord Vishnu. Gyanendra, they thought, did not embody the same kingly qualities. Furthermore, his son Paras, the new crown prince, had earned a bit of a reputation for debauchery. His misdeeds included several drunk driving accidents and firing weapons at random events for no reason.[9] Paras was no incarnation of Vishnu. How could he be king?

Paras never became king, of course. The monarchy fell during Gyanendra's reign. The Maoists emerged victorious at the end of the civil war, and Gyanendra was officially stripped of his major powers by the Parliament on June 10, 2006. He remained the royal figurehead for another two years before Nepal officially transitioned to a secular republic.[10]

In those five years, I saw the political axiom of my orbit completely transformed. Gyanendra's reign was our first experience with absolute authoritarianism. It's not that the government or the monarchy had been free of authoritarian conduct before Gyanendra, but rather that his forefathers had been clever enough to keep their authority outside of the noses of the Kathmandu elite.

Gyanendra broke the propaganda machine.

As soon as he became king, he initiated a curfew across Kathmandu, with shoot-on-sight orders for anyone who left their homes. Many communities across the city were already soured on him because of the chaos and the conspiracies around his reign. However, it was Gyanendra who turned the elite classes against himself. Within a few years of his tenure, the Maoists gained a lot of followers across the country. The royal massacre was a divine gift to their political cause. This random event had caused massive unrest in the capital city, leaving a power vacuum the CPN-M was all too eager to fill. They now had unexpected allies within pockets of Kathmandu elites, including other mainstream political parties such as the Nepal Congress.[11] Gyanendra was certainly not tuned out of these shifting tides, nor was he unaware of his immense unpopularity among the Nepali people. He saw the writing on the wall and did what any dictator fearful of the collapse of his reign would do: he exercised total control of all aspects of social, political, and economic life in Nepal.

In 2005 Gyanendra declared that Nepal would revert to an absolute monarchy, and the king would reign supreme over all matters.[12] During this period the discourse in my orbit started

to subtly shift. At parties people now discussed the incompeten-
cies of the new king, blaming him for the supposed bombings of safe tempos and movie theaters. The *maobadi* never
dared to attack our own capital city under the rule of great king
Birendra. Gyanendra did not know how to protect us. Occasionally, I began to hear some contrarian cousin or another point
out that the *maobadi* may not be the biggest threat to our lives.
Once I even heard someone mention that one of the leaders of
the movement, Baburam Bhattrai, had a PhD. The argument
they were trying to make was that maybe the Maoists were not
simply foolish savages causing destruction in their wake for no
reason. Maybe they had a plan.

I was absolutely perplexed by this knowledge about the creden-
tials of Bhattrai, whose given name Baburam I had heard uttered
countless times in my life with utter disdain. He, along with his
coleader and eventual president of Nepal in 2008 Prachanda, per-
sonified the comic book villain archetype in my mind. But this
particular bit of knowledge did not add up for me because my
whole life I had also been told that the most honorable achieve-
ment a person could attain in a lifetime was a doctoral degree.
Clearly, I have internalized that message. As an adult operating
in the academic space, I recognize that a PhD mostly indicates
a combination of privilege and a high tolerance for pain. But as
a child I was made to believe that such high levels of education
indicated the degree-owner was a chosen messiah of the universe.

Perhaps it was this internal inconsistency in the propaganda I
received that ultimately made me ask this question: Why would
someone with so much education act so foolishly? I have had
to revisit this premise over and over again throughout my personal and scholarly life. Over time, I had to let assumption after
assumption fall until only the why of it was left. I was assuming
that the Maoist movement was foolish because that is what my

social and political orbit told me. I was assuming that education denoted wisdom because that is what my social and political orbit told me. That simply left me with: *Why did a civil war
break out in my country?* The pages in this book don't even begin
to answer that question, but one thing is clear: the answer impli-
cates me and my loved ones. As a famous American singer once
said: "It's me, hi! I'm the problem, it's me!"

Unfortunately, it was not this particular realization that made
the tides turn in favor of the revolution within my community.
The authoritarian buffoonery of Gyanendra was mostly responsible. I remember the day when sentiments about the police
began to shift in my neighborhood of Old Baneshwor Height. It
is a small neighborhood atop a hill located minutes from the city
center that is primarily populated by brahmin families. Everyone
knew each other, and we often had lengthy conversations with
our neighbors from our rooftops.

When a member of our community got shot to death by a
police officer because he had been seen walking outside during
Gyanendra's first curfew in 2001, we were suddenly afraid of the
police. Hate festered underneath the fear, but the fear was para-
mount. Nobody broke curfew again. The man named Pashupati
Lohani simply wanted to get some fresh air and did not even go
down the hill. The cop had found him outside his own house
when he was killed. Yes, this kind of treatment of ordinary civil-
ians was commonplace outside Kathmandu—or perhaps in city
"neighborhoods" where unhoused *sukumbasi* communities lived,
which was mainly along the banks of the heavily polluted Bag-
mati River—but such violence was inconceivable in Baneshwor
Height. In an ironic twist, Lohani was a retired member of the
Nepali police force. Nobody was safe anymore.

For the first time, people in my neighborhood were forced to
consider what the police and the government were capable of

doing to maintain power. Moreover, the many curfews between 2001 and 2006 forced my community to do nothing but stay trapped in our homes to ponder the implications of this for week after week. As they discussed their insights with their neighbors from the rooftops, this *baun* community underwent a political awakening of its own. Their politics had little to do with the state's human rights abuses against oppressed castes in rural communities. Nonetheless, the conclusions that were drawn benefited the Maoist movements: Gyanendra is a tyrant, and all cops are bastards.

The tyrant was blind to the impact his extreme methods were having on communities that he previously had in his pocket. At every turn, he doubled and tripped down with more authority and more control. In April 2006, violent protests began to consume the city centers of Kathmandu.[13] The government responded with maximum state violence, sending in military forces to neutralize the protestors and using brutal tactics including shooting, tear gas, and bombings. To further dissuade people from joining the protests, Gyanendra instated another round of curfews. Nepal police were again ordered to shoot on sight anyone who broke curfew, and many police officers had in the preceding years shown how trigger-happy they could be.[14] Individual cops had the option to perhaps not shoot people for roaming outside their own homes, but at least in my neighborhood this was not the route they took. And that gives me little hope for what happened in other places.

There was certainly some amount of victim-blaming going around in the discourse, at least in the early years of the curfews. "He shouldn't have left his house!" "He broke the law!" people said about Lohani from my neighborhood. But as years passed, bringing more restraint, more curfews, more attacks on everyday freedoms of Nepali elites, even the staunchest supporters of the government became restless.[15] Everyone was scared and bored; never having experienced the ugly combination of those emotions, any remaining supporters of the king vanished as though they had never existed.

By this time in 2006, everyone in my neighborhood was political. Rooftop conversations had completely transformed: "Have you seen the news?" "The army shot at hundreds of people protesting the king, hospitals are overwhelmed!" I am ashamed to report that it was around this time that I realized things were really serious. Upon learning about the mass shootings and killings of protesters across Kathmandu by the military, it became impossible for me to ignore the violent process of history unfolding. At first when the curfews returned in 2006, I was simply relieved that I didn't have to go to school. That's a lie; actually, I was thrilled. Stay home all day? In my room? On my computer? I was about to become the most obedient citizen in the history of the kingdom. But even I got bored pretty quickly.

Although the early vibes were extremely bleak, soon enough the vibes took on a different, more revolutionary quality. Over these years, the king took everything from us, and all that was left was rooftop chatter. The collective sound echoing loudly through Baneshwor Height was a cacophony of pure rage: Gyanendra had to go. Every day for months in April 2006 we made sure to meet our neighbors on the rooftops, and every single house in our neighborhood joined the revolution. We made a lot of noise. Our whole neighborhood would be on their rooftops for hours with steel spoons banging on steel plates (steel dishware is common in Nepali households). My parents banged on the plates, and I banged on the plates too. It was exhilarating. I did not learn about the concept of collective effervescence until much later in my college sociology classes, but I lived that concept for a week.

Amid all the anger and the despair, there were also glimpses of joy. It was a peculiar sort of joy, almost other-worldly. I have not felt that particular feeling many times in my life. But in those days of the rooftop rebellion, it was almost as if I was feeling the excitement of every single person in my neighborhood all at once in my own body. Gyanendra had caged us in our own homes and cut us off from the rest of the world. We were going to end him with all this noise. We—the dominant-caste residents of Baneshwor Height—not the militant revolutionaries that had been fighting a whole war for a decade. Not the protestors out on the streets of the city centers getting shot and tear gassed at that very moment. Us with our plates and spoons and chants and collective rage in our relatively safe and comfortable homes. We were the superheroes we had thought the cops were all along.

The only other time I had thought things were really serious was about a year before the 2006 curfews when one day I tried to log on to the internet and it was gone. I went through many stages of grief that day, February 1, 2005. There was obviously something wrong with the landline. *The phone lines can barely withstand a gentle gush of rain! Why won't my mom just upgrade to broadband like people at school have? This is all her fault!* No matter how many times I plugged it off and on, the phone remained completely quiet, indistinguishable from any other object, no more interesting than the smelly old shoes it sat next to on the shoe rack. As hours passed, it became clear that the government had shut down the internet. Well, that can't apply to us! Maybe if I clean my room my mom will make a call to Mukesh or my uncle Durganath Sharma, the chief executive of NTV, and they will take care of this! As we conferred with our neighbors over the next day, I learned that the internet shutdown was indefinite. Nobody knew when it was going to come back. I cried in my bed all day. I didn't even get a chance to share this with anyone on the forums. It was a close friend's birthday, and I was supposed to make her a "birthday thread" that I had been working on all week. She would be so disappointed. There were new reviews on the fan fiction chapter I had posted that I couldn't open the night before because the internet was so slow; I had given up after trying for hours, knowing the reviews would still be there tomorrow. I was going to miss the "forum awards" happening in a few days, and I was nominated for so many categories. For the first time in my life, the war had affected me. My world had ended.

The rest of my family was also freaking out. The TV wasn't working, the landline wasn't working, my mom's Nokia 3310 wasn't working. The adults were really angry, and I overheard heated phone calls made to important people in important places. And it worked! We did it. Within a week, I got my internet back! The week was a minor glitch. I was excited to move on with my "life" and explain to my online friends why I was gone for so long. In the early 2000s forum culture timeline, one week was basically a whole year. I had a lot to catch up on. I wonder if any of my friends had more questions about the literal revolution going on in my country, because I don't think I told them much beyond "We have this awful king and he shut off the internet. So anyways, sorry I haven't updated the fan fiction in a week."

At the time, it was impossible for me to appreciate the remarkable reality that I was responding to one of the first mass-scale historic shutdowns of internet and mobile services by an authoritarian regime. Ang et al. describe Gyanendra's telecommunications shutdown as "a natural experiment to look at the impact of mobile phones" on revolutionary movements.[16] To my teenage self's blissful ignorance, the experiment focused largely on mobile telephony rather than on internet services. Landline services returned within days, and the internet followed shortly thereafter. These were the only two services I was concerned about. I would not have my own mobile phone until later in the year after finishing tenth grade. Thus it didn't particularly bother me that mobile services remained shut off for months.

My mom and her influential social circle, however, definitely noticed when their cell phones remained shut off. Where there was any room left, Gyanendra's remaining shreds of reputation among the Kathmandu elite were severely damaged by his decision to control communication technologies. Although mobile phones had existed for over a decade, in the early 2000s they were first becoming available for everyday use in Nepal. They became very popular in Kathmandu rather quickly.[17] The internet was also gaining popularity, but only among a specific subset of the Nepali population. Using the internet had many barriers to entry: access to a computer and dial-up networks, literacy, and technology and education, to name a few obvious barriers. Aside from some elite folks with fancy jobs in my mom's generation, the internet was most accessible and intuitive to people like me: upper-class millennials who were in their early teenage years. My mom, for example, never really used the internet until the advent of smartphones and Web 2.0.

For over a decade before the iPhone changed how mobile phones and the internet are used, mobile telephones were considered revolutionary technology by people who had access to them.[18] Gyanendra took this "revolutionary" concept quite literally and imagined that shutting mobile phones down would stop Maoist activity and Maoist propaganda from reaching the capital. As with many of his plans, this attempt fully backfired. In their study, Ang et al. conclude that mobile phones may not have been the main source of Gyanendra's downfall, but shutting them down was a major catalyst in ending his reign.[19]

This all goes back to the idea that elites in Kathmandu were never overtly political even though covertly they supported the regime and especially law enforcement until things changed. Their support for these institutions—and opposition to the *maobadi*—reflected their own interests and the pro-government, pro-police propaganda they encountered in their everyday lives. By taking away their cell phones—in addition to other extreme totalitarian measures such as curfews—they forced my community to shockingly choose the side of the insurgents. Gyanendra took something from us: something so small in the grand scheme of things, it was just cell phones. Yet in doing so, he ensured that for the first time in the history of our nation, our interests were aligned with the oppressed masses rather than with the status quo.

Gyanendra's "natural experiment" had failed, and it cost him the crown. The threat he perceived from the revolutionary potential of ICTs moved him to take authoritarian measures that reflected the possibilities in Nepal in early 2000s. The internet returned quickly because people like me, elite teenagers, were not perceived as a threat. The last ICT to be restored was the more affordable prepaid cell phones, the communication tool most accessible to the working classes and masses of the oppressed castes. At this point in history, most cell phones only included talk and text functions. The big innovations in the technology were upgrade to "color phones" with games and videorecording possibilities. Most people in Nepal used black and white Nokia phones, which offered the surprisingly addictive game of "Snake" plus talk and text.

All this is to say that at the time of the Nepali revolution there weren't many creative ways for an authoritarian government to engage ICTs as counterrevolutionary tactics. Gyanendra intervened in the only way he could, by cutting off connectivity entirely. Even to this day, many authoritarian regimes model Gyanendra's approach by shutting down mobile phone and internet services. In the last two decades, thanks to Web 2.0, the attention economy, and the ability for states to buy user-data for surveillance, counterinsurgent strategies have evolved far beyond what Gyanendra's regime could imagine.

# 4

# SOCIAL MOVEMENTS, COUNTER MOVEMENTS, AND DISCOURSE IN THE ATTENTION ECONOMY

In academic and policy settings, information and communications technology for development (ICT4D) is among the most prominent narratives about how modern communication technologies can save the world. I have identified many flaws in the ICT4D framework, and in this chapter I draw your attention to another prominent narrative about ICTs and global transformation: social movements. In general, scholarly literature on ICTs and social movements involves more critical debates about the success of ICTs compared to the development literature, which tends to collectively support the premise of ICT4D, with notable exceptions.[1] Surprisingly, scholarship on ICT4D and ICTs and social movements do not tend to be in conversation with one another.

However, it is undeniable that both frameworks share a central premise: the notion that we can harness modern communication technologies for societal progress. The ICT4D literature identifies how technology can save disempowered populations, whereas the social movements literature identifies how disempowered populations can draw on ICTs to save themselves. At the outset, it appears that using ICTs for social movements takes the focus away from how elites use ICTs for progress and toward a narrative of self-determinism for the masses of disempowered people. However, a closer look at social movements that have succeeded with the expansion of the internet reveals the difficulties in escaping elite imaginations.[2]

Early proponents of ICTs for social movements emphasized the notion of "horizontal communication" as the foundation that allows mass mobilization against structures of power in ways that were unimaginable prior to modern communication technologies.[3] The premise of horizontal communication is simple: because the internet theoretically removes various social barriers to distant and large-scale communication (while also forgoing the governing structures of traditional offline societies), the nature of informational exchange online is collective and not hierarchical. Prior breakthroughs in communication technologies supported more vertical forms of exchange. For example, television and "mainstream" news media allowed the government and media forces to unidirectionally provide "information" to the masses. Without the ability to directly communicate with these sources of information, it was easy to succumb to various forms of propaganda. In contrast, the internet allows for masses to communicate "information" to one another within and outside the context of state forces and media corporations, removing the hierarchical nature of information transfers of technologies of the past.

When it comes to social movements, many scholars believed that such horizontalism allows for improvements in the ways masses mobilize for collective action. The most frequently cited evidence for the merits of horizontalism on social movements is the success of several antiauthoritarian revolutions that occurred across countries in the Middle East in the early 2010s, collectively known as "the Arab Spring." In 2010 in Tunisia, a street vendor named Mohamed Bouazizi self-immolated due to the extreme economic hardships he experienced under the authoritarian regime of Zine El Abidine Ben Ali.[4] This act of radical defiance was caught on a mobile video camera and quickly went viral across Tunisia. The response was an enraged Tunisian population that orchestrated large-scale protests that ended with the resignation of Ben Ali and the theoretical end to authoritarian regimes in Tunisia. The revolution then began to cascade across other Middle Eastern countries including Egypt and Libya.[5]

Nonetheless, the premise of horizontalism has earned criticism in more recent years. If we look closely at the Arab Spring movements, the struggle for power between masses and the authoritarian governments often manifested in a cat-and-mouse game of rapid online mobilization on the side of the masses and media surveillance and control tactics on the side of the government. For example, Hosni Mubarak's government in Egypt shut down the internet during the Tahrir Square protests in 2011.[6] Telecommunications infrastructure, including internet and phone lines, are provided either by government services directly or by powerful private and multinational corporations that are all too eager to work with the government. Most countries have some form of government telecommunications service, and in many countries governments engage public-private partnerships with national and multinational telecommunications corporations. When governments lack direct authority over telecommunications services, they can work with big tech firms to trade surveillance data in the attention economy.

## MECHANISMS OF CONTROL

In authoritarian settings, controlling access to media often serves as the first line of defense in preventing the masses from communicating during periods of civil unrest. Growing up in Nepal during the Nepali Civil War, I experienced the impacts of such authoritarian tactics firsthand. I can trace my interests in political economy almost precisely to the years of the civil war. To understand why my most precious resource was being taken away from me, I had to learn about the world outside of my walls. What I found was that the king took extreme measures to control all communication so that the Maoist insurgents would be limited in their operations. At that time mobile telephony was just becoming mainstream, and social media was limited to the niche interests of quirky teenagers on forums and Myspace. Authoritarian regimes feared and revered the possibilities presented by these technologies. Gyanendra blocked telecommunications services in spite of the fact that the Maoist insurgents were skeptical of state-owned media and forged their own communication networks.[7] In the decades that followed, authoritarian pushback against online protest mobilization have become substantially more aggressive across the world, as the mass surveillance apparatus expanded within a marketplace of attention.

With Web 2.0 came the widespread popularity of social media websites such as Facebook and X. Facebook, especially when combined with the iPhone, changed everything. Soon after, there was a removal of distinction between internet and reality; there was only hyperreality. The French sociologist Jean Baudrillard used the term "hyperreality" to describe the postmodern mutation of reality as an elusive concept only expressed through symbolic simulations such as art and images.[8] Reality itself is altered in the process of symbolic reproduction. Mark Fisher draws from this concept in *Capitalist Realism* to describe modern life represented through the media in the capitalist world of neoliberal imaginaries.[9] The concept of hyperreality perfectly encapsulates life post–Web 2.0 and social media. *If a tree falls in the woods but nobody posts a picture on Instagram, does the tree exist?*

By the time I moved to the United States for my undergraduate degree in 2009, I did not feel that using social media was a choice. All my friends back home were on it, and slowly my cousins and even some older family members began to join. If I wanted to stay connected to my people in Nepal in a convenient way, I had to fully embrace Facebook. In my sophomore year at college, I remember writing an essay about the merits and threats of Facebook, emphasizing its unbelievable global reach with nearly five hundred million users. Today Facebook has nearly three billion active monthly users.[10]

As a global phenomenon, Facebook is credited by many scholars of the Arab Spring movement as the key space for social movement activity. In particular, many scholars cite a Facebook group called "We Are All Khaled Said" as a major catalyst for the Egyptian revolution in 2011 because nearly a third of the protesters in Tahrir Square stated they first heard about the mobilizations through Facebook.[11] Unprepared to deal with these new forms of mobilization, the authoritarian government led by Hosni Mubarak took a page from Gyanendra's playbook and initiated a media blackout. Gyanendra was among the first authoritarian leaders to set the media blackout precedent in the ICT environment.

History repeated itself. Just as Gyanendra's choices to disconnect media access contributed to his downfall, Mubarak's choices contributed to his eventual resignation. Many scholars suggest that middle- and upper-class Egyptians took to the streets and joined the protesters in Tahrir Square after the five-day internet shutdown.[12] Perhaps counterinsurgents began to learn some lessons around this time. Shutting down internet and mobile services always had the potential to backfire.

In the decade following the Arab Spring movement, governments have steered in a different direction: rather than cut access to ICT, they increasingly seek to control ICTs by working with big tech firms.

From a world-systems perspective, the key role of the state within the capitalist world-system is to protect the interest of firms and corporations and enable the free flow of capital across geographic units. As Wallerstein writes: "The relationship of states to firms is a key to understanding the capitalist world economy."[13] Within a world-systemic framework, the state supports the goal of endless accumulation driven by firms by exercising laws to externalize the cost of production to society. In traditional economies, for example, society undertakes the burden of living with the toxicity produced by chemical factory operations, or society deals with the problem of material resource exhaustion. An additional mechanism through which the state supports capital accumulation is by monopolizing "lawful" use of violence to mitigate threats against ruling classes and corporate interests.[14] The state's role in exercising legitimized authority and violence whenever it seems necessary to protect ruling interests is crucial to understanding the relationship between firms and states in the attention economy.

The internet is the ultimate surveillance apparatus.[15] States today can monitor the activities of their citizenry more closely and easily than ever before. Fuchs unpacks the political economy of Web 2.0, identifying two forms of surveillance particular to the attention economy: economic surveillance and political surveillance.[16] Economic surveillance is how the attention economy generates capital by monitoring user data. Political surveillance is when firms and the state employ user data to monitor and stifle resistance and dissent.

At the world-systemic level, an interplay between these two forms of surveillance in the attention economy supports the goal of unfettered capital accumulation, especially in a time of waning material resources. Firms monetize attention across the whole world to extract wealth and maintain the economic system, and both firms and states use the same wealth (or data) to monitor and thwart resistance against the system. In many cases, dissent is stifled *within* the attention economy, i.e., online through either censorship or new forms of social capital imposed directly by firms. For example, the big tech firm Meta Platforms Inc. engages in direct censorship on its social media platform Facebook by deleting politically threating posts, including calls for uprisings against the Israeli occupation of Palestine.[17] Meta Platforms Inc. further promotes censorship by indirectly encouraging self-censorship as a mechanism of maintaining social capital—i.e., Facebook is a social space in which people desire social capital via "likes" and other such social currency.[18] Such an online-first strategy of political surveillance is especially effective when rising tides of dissent are likely to be nonviolent and are not immediately threatening.

Political surveillance turns into state intervention when dissent within the attention economy threatens to take on more violent or threatening qualities *offline*. Before this point, the state has little need to directly intervene. But once dissent begins to threaten state power—and thus the capitalist world-system it protects—the state can use the attention economy data for surveillance and respond accordingly with offline violence to stifle such forms of resistance. For example, in an analysis of the conflict in Syria, Anita Ghodes found that higher internet connectivity correlated with higher instances of targeted, violent repression—including disappearing and death—of individuals and groups that posed violent threats to the authoritarian regime. Ghodes writes: "The collection of highly specified intelligence on the intentions and location of critical players in antigovernment movements enables state violence to be more targeted and tailored toward individuals."[19]

Controlling media through propaganda has always been hugely successful in the "old media" environments of newspapers and television. In Edward Herman and Noam Chomsky's popular text *Manufacturing Consent*, they outline several filters through which "news" is processed in traditional media ecosystems. One of their key ideas is that corporations control media sources, and their PR teams work with governments to decide what is "news."[20] Newer studies have tried to apply these ideas to ICTs and uncover new ways for the propaganda machine to operate.[21] One example of such propaganda is astroturfing on social media sites such as X, i.e., flooding the site with planted users that support a government's position. These strategies were used, for example, in 2019 by Narendra Modi's Hindu nationalist government in India.[22] As the nation protested Modi's Citizenship Amendment Act (CAA)—which explicitly excluded Muslims from citizenship eligibility in India—investigators discovered that Modi's party flooded X with supporters of CAA to neutralize emerging dissent on social media.

## ICTs MODERATE STATE VIOLENCE IN SOCIAL MOVEMENTS

To unpack these connections between ICTs, states, and social movements, I draw from the *Mass Mobilizations Data Project*. The role of the state is to protect the interests of firms and capital, so states can intervene when the system poses serious threats. Here I define serious threats as protests that are violent in nature. From the U.S. Civil War to the Arab Spring, and my own experience growing up during the Nepali Civil War, history has shown that violent protests are likely to threaten the state and create revolutionary change at the level of the state. In the world-systems framework, seeking state power is considered by many scholars to be the first step in abolishing the capitalist world-system.[23] The first step is to assume state power, and the second step is to change the laws and systems put in place by the state to protect capital.

Historically, powerful groups have prepared for such alterations by monopolizing legitimized authority. In particular, states rely on their law enforcement and military wings to stifle violent tides of dissent with revolutionary potential. This is what happened in Nepal when I was growing up, and this is why the United States has a massive military and policing budget today. As Frantz Fanon writes in the *Wretched of the Earth*: "The colonial world is a world cut in two. The dividing line, the frontiers are shown by barracks and police stations. In the colonies it is the policeman and the soldier who are the official, instituted go-betweens, the spokesmen of the settler and his rule of oppression."[24]

State violence is a critical tool that has been used against social movements historically as well as today. With ICTs and the attention wing of the propaganda machine, what has changed is *when* state violence is needed. Today, many users' behaviors—including dissent—are controlled within the attention economy itself using various tactics from astroturfing to censorship to self-censorship. This kind of nonviolent control is especially effective for online-only movements. However, when movements take a violent turn offline, states must violently intervene to stifle them. To demonstrate these processes across countries and over-time,

I share some findings from my panel data analysis of the *Mass Mobilizations Data Project* for 153 countries from 1990 to 2017 that reinforce these ideas.

In spite of the challenges associated with measuring the attention economy quantitatively, there is tremendous value in utilizing close proxy measures to understand patterns across nations and over time. Thus, in my study, I use two measures of ICT that approximate exposure to the attention economy at different levels. Data on percent of mobile subscribers approximates the percent of the population with *low levels of exposure* to the attention economy. Until the year 2007 when the first iPhone appeared, mobile phones did not prominently feature internet connectivity. Smartphones are a relatively new phenomena, and this study covers ICT penetration since 1990. For more than half of the years covered here, mobile phones were similar to landlines but carried two innovative features: mobility and text-based communication. With the rapid rise in popularity of smartphones after 2007, more people with mobile phones are now exposed to the attention economy via mobile subscriptions; however, major inequality remains in (1) access to smartphones over older technology and (2) the ability to pay for internet and data features among lower income populations. Thus mobile phone subscriptions on the whole capture lower levels of exposure to the attention economy.

In contrast, data on the percent of broadband internet users shows *high levels of exposure* to the attention economy. This measure directly captures the global population that is online. In fact, even populations with smartphones often rely on broadband and wi-fi connections over mobile subscription and data to use internet and social media sites, visit forums, conduct search functions, and engage a wide variety of activities and "discourse" that translate their "clicks" into monetizable data.

Through these proxies, I evaluate how the attention economy streamlines simultaneous interventions at the levels of state power and discourse to differentially address movements that pose different levels of threats to the capitalist world-system. The outcome of interest is a binary indicator of whether or not there were violent protests in a country-year. Furthermore, I use another binary indicator of whether or not a state responded violently to protests in a given country-year unit. By analyzing the binary indicator of protester violence with proxies for the attention economy (mobile phones and internet), I am able to investigate whether the attention economy moderates the likelihood of a violent state response depending on the nature of the protests (violent versus nonviolent).

At high levels of attention economy exposure, nonviolent protests that gain visibility in online discourse can be stifled online through the power of algorithms and big tech firms. In other words, if a movement is popular online but has nonthreatening offline activity, the state does not need to intervene: the intervention can happen fully online at the level of discourse within the attention economy itself. However, if a movement is violent—i.e., there is threatening offline activity—the state can step in to respond with violence and severity. Furthermore, if this reasoning holds, at lower levels of attention economy exposure there is less opportunity to intervene at the level of online discourse, so there may be a higher likelihood of a violent response from the state *both* for violent and nonviolent protests.

Figures 4.1 and 4.2 plot the moderating effects of mobile phone subscriptions and internet use, respectively, on the relationship between protester violence and state violence. Figure 4.1 shows that across 153 countries over twenty-seven years, as the percent of people with mobile subscriptions increased, more states were likely to respond violently to violent protests (controlling

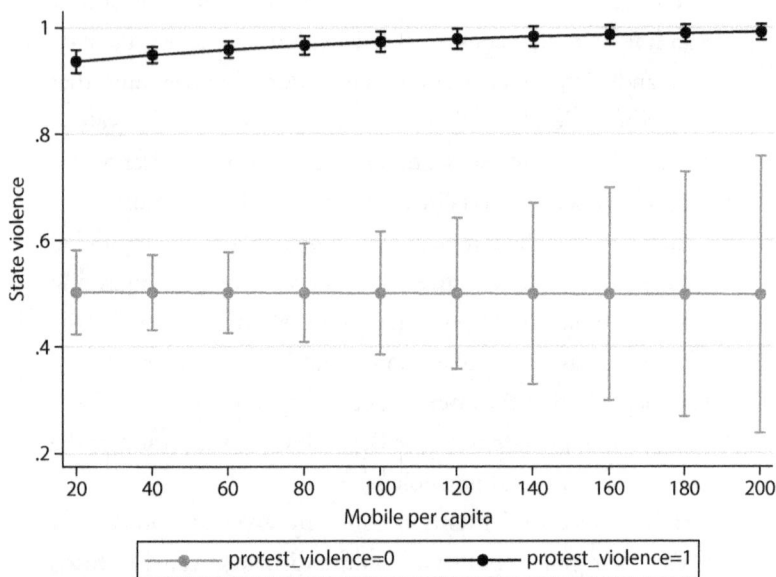

**FIGURE 4.1** Predicted probabilities for state violence across percent of mobile subscriptions, 1990 to 2018.

for all other relevant factors). However, as more people used mobile phones, nonviolent protests had no relationship with state violence. At first this pattern may not seem particularly noteworthy, but when we contrast it with figure 4.2, an intriguing narrative emerges.

Figure 4.2 shows that, across the same countries over the same years, as the percent of people using the internet increased, more states were likely to respond violently to violent protests. This is congruent with the results for mobile phones. Where the patterns become especially illuminating is when we note the moderating effects of internet use on nonviolent protests and the state response. Namely, as the percent of people using the internet increased across these countries and over time, the likelihood of

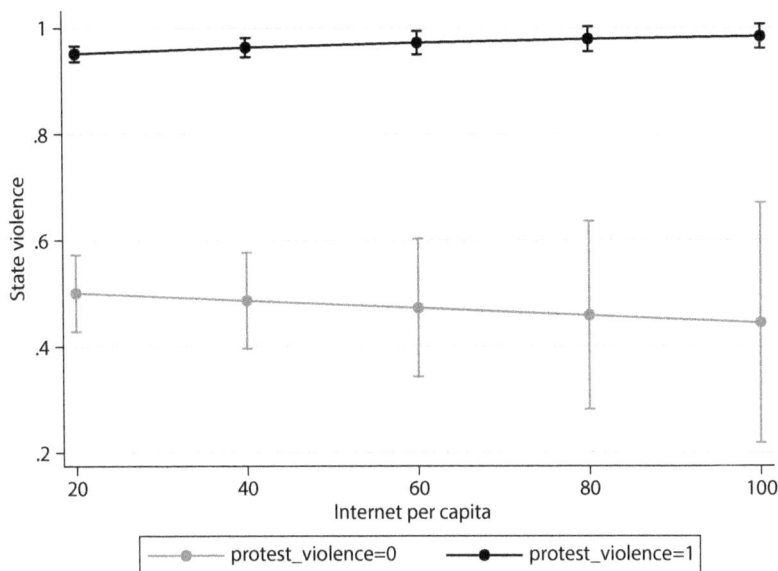

**FIGURE 4.2** Predicted probabilities for state violence across the percent of internet users, 1990 to 2018.

a violent state response *decreased* for nonviolent protests. In other words, as more people used the internet globally, fewer states responded violently to nonviolent protests.

These findings support the idea that high levels of attention economy exposure through internet use subjects the user to behavioral control within the attention economy itself. Through these various mechanisms, firms and states can work together to monitor nonthreatening dissent and use control tactics from astroturfing to self-censorship to neutralize dissent. Violence is not necessary. At low levels of attention economy exposure, however, it is more difficult to engage those mechanisms of control.

Without internet connectivity, mobile phone users are limited in how they organize, and at the same time, states and firms are limited in what they can monitor and control. The fewer features mobile users can access, the greater their need is to engage more fully in social movements. States can monitor phone calls and text messages and utilize geo-tracking technology to identify violent dissent and respond appropriately with violent interventions. However, tracking phone calls, text messages, and locations may be insufficient to (1) identify nonviolent protest activity and to (2) intervene creatively to stifle such activity within the attention economy. These are some ways I interpret the lack of a clear moderating effect of mobile phone subscriptions on protester violence and state response. In light of a clearly visible decreasing effect of the internet on nonviolent protests and state violence, these interpretations are plausible.

## CULTURAL POLITICAL ECONOMY
## AND DISCOURSE

To understand the nature of online interventions to stifle social movements, it is important to unpack a critical aspect of the average online experience: exposure to discourse. From the perspective that attention-time is a form of work, curating discourse is the direct product of that work (among other products). What exactly is discourse in the context of international political economy? The framework of the cultural political economy (CPE) helps us unpack the political economic elements of discourse.

CPE is a framework that infuses cultural and semiotic analyses within economic and political contexts by neither minimizing the salience of material reality nor underplaying the role of culture and meaning-making in developing social formations.[25] CPE treats economic, political, and cultural forces as co-evolving mechanisms that operate together to describe and explain social reality. Within this framework, social realities, specifically *economic systems*, emerge at the nexus of various visions and interests—"imaginaries"—pushed by groups and institutions with varying levels of power to realize them. The economic imaginary of capitalism emerges against potentially competing economic imaginaries because elite economic and political forces develop, design, and legitimize the economic processes and activities that construct and reinforce the cultural zeitgeist. These forces (e.g., multinational corporations, core nations, the World Bank) determine the boundaries of cultural discourse. By controlling institutions that provide knowledge and education, they have a great influence on what constitutes a culture. Within this structure, mass media—the social institution incorporating ICTs—serves to navigate between competing imaginaries to generate necessary support from social actors at various levels of power to determine which ideas are infused into the discourse of a given cultural landscape.

To unpack the relationships between firms, states, and discourse, I specifically draw upon the agency, structure, institutions, and discourse (ASID) approach "to understand socioeconomic development." Moulaert et al. posit that rather than a binary structure/agency model, socioeconomic development can most robustly be understood by addressing the agentic "actions" that impact a process of development, the "structures" that limit or expand those actions, the "institutions" that promote or hinder actions and navigate between actions and structures, and the "discourse" that encompasses interactions between and across these three elements of society.[26]

The ASID framework—a CPE effort—can be applied to understanding how the attention economy and states influence social movements at the discursive level. "Agency" operates at the individual level of ICT users, who have the theoretical volition to direct their attention wherever they choose: in terms of social movements, potential participants have the agency to decide which movements to focus on in a digital landscape full of competing movements with different goals and interests. The theoretical volition is first complicated at the level of "structures" because in ICTs there are literal structures in place in the form of platforms and algorithms. These structures moderate what is visible to each individual user, limiting the possibilities of social movements (among a theoretically infinite pool of available movements) in which an individual could choose to participate.

The structures, of course, are deliberately designed and implemented by specific "institutions" with specific interests. When it comes to social media, these institutions are powerful profit-oriented corporations such as Apple Inc. and Meta Platforms Inc. that ultimately serve to maintain the U.S. economic hegemony. Alternatively, institutions such as ByteDance Ltd. support rising hegemonic competitors such as China. The United States and China are by far the largest market shareholders in the attention economy, and both nations have strong states that protect their firms. The United States covertly maintains authority with a militant law enforcement wing and the largest military apparatus in history. China is overtly authoritarian. The corporations protected by these states have the most influence over the structure of ICT platforms, and by extension they have considerable influence on individual choices to participate in any social movement. Major corporations and states represent key institutions that influence movements that organize using ICTs. The influence of these institutions serve the persistence of the economic imaginary of the capitalist world-system.

Competing imaginaries from movement organizers are fueled by substantially less power. Without states to protect their alternative interests, social movements are minor institutions operating amorphously under disparate premises to compete for attention among online users. As long as these movements use platforms whose structures are controlled by major firms and powerful states, they operate within the boundaries of the economic imaginaries of the capitalist world-system. Some nonstate anarchist movements may overcome this limitation by opting for more diffused and decentralized technologies not bounded by these institutions (e.g. Signal). However, these movements face additional challenges in garnering individual attention because the pool of people to potentially mobilize is severely diminished.

Movements that continue to use the hegemonic online apparatus and work with a larger pool of potential activists struggle to succeed using hegemonic digital structures. Economic and political surveillance, as discussed previously, work to stifle dissent via online censorship or through state-led violence depending on the severity of threats presented. At the cultural level, dissent is further mitigated through a combination of (1) self-censorship in pursuit of social capital in online social networks and (2) algorithmic manipulations in online discourse. Social networks can range from friends and families to celebrities and complete strangers. These networks post, repost, and share ideas, opinions, humor, outrage, and all variety of emotional and intellectual content that makes up a user's online experience within the confines of the structures put in place by corporations. Such content is what ultimately amounts to the "discourse" that is visible and accessible to each individual user online in the attention economy.

Discourse, thus, is what exists after all the agents, structures, and institutions have yielded relative influence and power over online communication. The relative power of firms that design ICT platforms and algorithms is by far the largest group, but using CPE we can understand how this power is not the sole contributor to online discourse. Competing institutions may exert different levels of power to push competing agendas. If those competing institutions present little to no threat to the capitalist world-system, little to no state intervention is necessary; however, if serious threat is detected by the surveillance apparatus, states can intervene violently.

To provide one concrete example of how this plays out, consider Indigenous imaginaries. In stark contrast to the imaginary of the capitalist world-system that destroys the natural environment for capital accumulation, many Indigenous imaginaries promote preservation of the natural environment and self-sustaining ecosystems. Antisystemic ideas around Indigenous land rights (that draw from competing Indigenous imaginaries) have successfully penetrated online discourse. We can observe this, for example, in the ongoing popular trend to include land acknowledgments in all kinds of discursive spaces in the United States, online and offline.[27] Land acknowledgment is a symbolic movement that does not automatically threaten the capitalist world-system even though the movement is rooted in support of alternative imaginaries. The United States does not need to violently respond to individuals and groups acknowledging the Indigenous tribes from whom specific units of US land were appropriated.

When the underlying alternative Indigenous imaginaries threaten the imaginaries of the capitalist world-system, however, the state engages in a violent response. This was most visible in the United States during the Indigenous-led protests against rerouting the Dakota Access Pipeline (DAPL) near the Standing Rock Sioux Reservation in 2016–17. In an effort to protect Indigenous land from fossil fuel industry exploitation that would create a water crisis in the reservation while also destroying spaces of historical and spiritual significance, this protest drew historic numbers of Indigenous protesters and allies. Online, the hashtag #NoDAPL was trending in discourse, and offline protesters used tactics such as chaining themselves to heavy machinery to impede construction.[28] The state used its law enforcement wing to violently intervene and protect the interests of the Dakota Access, LLC. Some of the violent state responses against protestors at Standing Rock included encampment by militarized police using attack dogs, tear gas, and water cannons during freezing weather conditions. The DAPL construction was successfully completed in April 2017.

The Standing Rock case demonstrates that social movements can garner attention in online cultural discourse despite the disproportionate influence of powerful structures and institutions. When the same movements engage offline organizational mechanisms that threaten the capitalist world-system, states violently intervene to protect the interests of firms. In contrast, when movements related to the same alternative imaginaries are not accompanied by threatening offline activity—as in the case of land acknowledgment statements—states can ignore them. Algorithmic structures may even support the popularity of such efforts within the discourse, and they might encourage strong emotional responses that—according to previous research—are associated with a higher likelihood of virality.[29] In other words, nonthreatening movements may serve to increase the currency of "likes" and "clicks" that build legitimate capital ripe for accumulation in the attention economy.

## CENTERING DISCOURSE IN THE WORLD ATTENTION ECONOMIC SYSTEM

World-systems perspectives engage social movements as mechanisms that work to alter the characteristics of the modern world-system. Pioneers of this theory point to the historic "world revolutions" of 1848 and the "European Spring" and the 1960s cultural revolutions in the United States and beyond to demonstrate how masses of people have come together to challenge elements of the capitalist world-system. Each revolutionary era witnessed massive changes in social, political, and economic aspects of the world-system. The 1848 revolutions witnessed a historical collapse of monarchies and subsequent democratization across Europe, and the 1960 U.S. revolutions witnessed the success of the civil rights and women's rights movements. Across countries and over time, early world-systems scholars emphasized the role of extant communication technologies in facilitating social movements: "The [concern] flagged in the [Communist] Manifesto, the material means of unity among those geographically separate, remains central. The means themselves, and the very form of their materiality, have been fundamentally transformed. More and more anti-systemic movements will find their own cohesion and coherence forged and destroyed by the newest of the means of mediating social relations."[30]

These words describe the impact of the once "cutting-edge" technological innovation of the television on social movements. In Marxist thought, including neo-Marxist perspectives such as world-systems analysis, the roles of technology and communication technologies are always emphasized as the means through which the masses across geographic regions could unite to access their visions for change. Such technologies become even more relevant when considering the world as a single economic system, where the roles of the dominant and subjugated become stratified along geographic zones separated by great physical distances. The innovation of the internet represents the ultimate theoretical possibility for uniting dispossessed masses across the global periphery.

In practice, however, the advent of such an unprecedented transformation in the ways people communicate across the world comes with challenges, such as the construction of an attention economic system. Beyond exploiting Global South populations to extract wealth for core nations, the attention economy further complicates the relationships of power across groups and nations. Traditional perspectives may not sufficiently account for these complications: the influence of culture on the internet, and vice versa. The online culture of the internet is a mutation of preexisting sociocultural relations in the offline world. Simply stated, when the internet came along, it's not as though all the subjugated people in the world were ready to revolutionize the moment they could instantly communicate with every person in the world. Today we can accomplish such an unimaginable feat of communication instantly with most people in the world. Yet the capitalist world-system continues its ruthless expansion as we quickly accelerate toward the end of the human race as we know it. The world-system uses the platforms where people publicly engage to extract wealth in a time of material resource exhaustion.

There are two additional considerations of note here. First, the internet is not a *passive* tool ready for use by the masses and molded solely to their will. The internet is unlike letters or landlines, which are still subjected to government surveillance but otherwise relatively independent of other influences. The internet is also unlike television, which serves as a highly effective propaganda tool due to its decidedly vertical nature of communication.[31] In this way television is relatively independent of the influence of the people in direct contrast to letters and landlines. The internet is not fully independent of the influence of anyone using the internet. The internet presents an active, evolving, and continuously transforming sphere of communication visible as discourse, which serves in a way as a separate little world-system of its own. This world-system has its own economy, as I have discussed, and it also has its own culture. Every user of the internet is influenced by the culture of the internet and influences the culture of the internet.

Second, the world systemic idea that the relationship of dominance and subjugation is mostly segregated along national lines is limited. Although it is undeniable that the core exploits the periphery to extract wealth for the project of unfettered capital accumulation, exploitation iterates in many other forms in our society. This idea is accepted in mainstream sociology and mainstream society: structures of power reproduce in many ways beyond economic relations, for example, racial, gender and caste-based inequality is pervasive across many countries and contexts within the world-system. To address both of these points we need to address an element of society that world-systems perspectives only minimally engages as an epiphenomenon of the capitalist world-system: culture. The sociologists Mueller and Schmidt propose that gaps in world-systems perspectives can be addressed by infusing cultural political economy frameworks.[32]

## MANUFACTURING THE ZEITGEIST

Cultural political economy allows us to engage in a more complete analysis of the capitalist world-system, especially as it relates to the internet and the attention economy. The CPE perspective treats culture and political economy as coevolving, mutually reinforcing elements that determine whose imaginations become a zeitgeist over competing imaginations for sociopolitical realities. In other words, culture and political economy work together to decide the characteristics of the world we live in, as well as how we engage with each other in that world. Bringing CPE perspectives within a world-systems framework is useful in unpacking the elusive phenomenon of virality, especially as it relates to social movements.

CPE embeds cultural analysis within economic and political contexts without minimizing the role of material reality or downplaying the significance of culture and meaning-making in creating social realities. Through this framework, we can think about social realities, and particularly economic systems, as emergent properties of multiple visions and interests intersecting at varying levels of power. Different groups, institutions, and individuals have disparate abilities to realize their own visions for society. Bob Jessop uses the concept of "imaginaries" to describe the various potential manifestations of the nature of social reality. "Imaginaries" describe potential sets of rules and aspirations that could govern the modalities of social reality.

The economic imaginary of capitalism emerges against potentially competing economic imaginaries because elite economic and political forces have disproportionately high levels of power to manifest their visions into social reality. These forces develop, design, and legitimize which economic processes and activities construct and reinforce the cultural zeitgeist. To exercise their influence on the emergent manifestation of society, core states and MNCs determine the boundaries of cultural discourse. They accomplish these goals by essentially controlling institutions that provide knowledge and education. Thus they have a great influence on what constitutes a culture. Studies within the world polity theory tradition—as discussed in previous chapters—present us with ample empirical support to demonstrate that the diffusion of cultural standards across the world follows a pattern set by elite institutions such as the UN and major INGOs.

Social movements seek either to change certain aspects of the capitalist world-system or to change the system of historical capitalism in favor of an entirely new system. Social movements grapple with the questions of *which imaginaries define social reality* and how to change the imaginaries to manifest new realities. They also navigate whether boundaries for changing imaginaries reside within or outside of the world capitalist economic system. Mass media, including the internet and modern ICTs, navigate between competing imaginaries to generate necessary support from social actors at various levels of power to determine which ideas are infused into the discourse of a given cultural landscape.

For social movements to succeed online—i.e., attain virality—they must garner adequate support from various interests at the micro-, meso-, and macrolevels of society with varying levels of power. Critically, they must receive favorable attention within the cultural zeitgeist and discourse. Any given imaginary can become the dominant mode of social reality only after legitimization in the dominant culture and discourse. If the dominant culture rejects a modality, it cannot manifest into reality. Yet the dominant culture tends to respond to existing political economic realities, and it often reinforces those imaginaries.

World-systems perspectives regard culture as an epiphenomena of political economy, which is used to identify how in modern day capitalism "neoliberalism" is the dominant ideology in a global "geoculture." This suggests that political economic forces unilaterally push for the dominant culture of neoliberalism, negating the role of cultural reproduction of neoliberalism through the zeitgeist. In his popular book *Capitalist Realism: Is There No Alternative?*, Mark Fisher draws from postmodern perspectives to describe how neoliberalism is inseparable from the cultural experience of lived realities within modern capitalist society.[33] Fisher uses popular culture examples to demonstrate how even creative media such as hip-hop or movies that present anticapitalist imaginaries and "challenge" neoliberalism are highly profitable enterprises. The idea of anticapitalism resonates with the culture, but the result is not a change away from capitalism. Instead there is an increase in consumption of anticapitalist art and increased market demands for anticapitalist media. Fisher uses these examples to make the case that, in essence, we are fish and neoliberalism is water. Far from an epiphenomenon pushed only from the top down, neoliberalism *is* culture. Neoliberalism *is* the zeitgeist. The CPE approach brings this reality into political economic analysis, emphasizing that change away from the political economic reality of capitalism is inseparable from the process of migrating to dry land.

## ANTI-FASCIST, PRO-CAPITALIST, NEOLIBERAL IMAGINARIES

In my study of protest participation across 141 countries over twenty-eight years, which was published in the *Journal of World Systems Research*, I noticed that internet and mobile phone expansion supported the success of certain types of movements, but potentially stifled other types of movements. Despite the general trajectory of increased protest participation with increased access to ICTs, I learned that patterns of change for various movements were unequal. There were also some differences in how access to mobile phones affected protests compared to internet use specifically. To understand the influence on different types of movements, I separated the protest movements by categories of "protester demands" and "protest group identity." This allowed me to identify how social movements with specific agendas supported by traditionally marginalized groups fared compared to other types of movements.

In general, access to the internet was more consistently associated with an increase in participation in protests when compared to mobile phones. This is an important point: while all connectivity supports social movements, having access to the *online world* on the internet fosters more protest engagement. Social media and the attention economy operate inside this world. Before the smartphone revolution, mobile phones were simply a more *mobile* extension of older communication technologies. As the technology expanded, communication technologies added features of text, image, and video messaging to mobile telephony. As digital inequality persists in many parts of the world, some people—especially people in rural areas of Global South countries—still remain connected through these simpler devices.[34] These populations are not yet fully integrated into the attention economy, and they serve as future potential sources of attention extraction to expand the attention market and generate more wealth for technology corporations in core countries.

The internet, of course, is the heart of the attention economy. It is home to the *online world* that has been such a big part of my life and personal experiences. Those who are online using the internet are almost certainly integrated into the attention economy. Even if one were to use the internet only to perform searches and find answers, these activities are tracked and sold by corporations such as Google LLC. Once we make it to the world of online, there is no escaping the attention economy. This world is where *discourse* takes place.

Platforms such as X and Reddit are where certain voices—and movements—garner lots of attention, and others fizzle out into an empty but watchful void. Social movement organizers navigate this void, hoping to mobilize participants against competing movements. For a movement to "succeed," in the sense of influencing large numbers of people to show up at *offline* protests, it must overcome two difficult challenges. First, it must become relevant in the discourse enough to earn the currency of attention. Second, it must survive the heat of the discourse to compel virtual onlookers to become protest participants.

To become relevant in discourse and earn visibility in the attention economy, social movements need to pass the ASID test. Social media forums provide live and active spaces to collectively express the kind of strong emotional reactions (discourse) that promote spontaneous protest participation. The interactive element of social media creates desirable spaces for organizers (institutions) to share their own news and propaganda using varieties of multimedia from blog posts to videos. Users can then collectively respond to this content, sharing emotional responses, and they may even form instantaneous bonds that mimic the kinds of bonds that were historically formed over time in traditional organizing spaces (agency). Finally, and most influentially, the social media algorithms (structures) that moderate discourse are designed by massive U.S. corporations such as Apple Inc. and Meta Platforms Inc., and they effectively control how content spreads and which type of content receives the most attention. These corporations represent institutions with more power than protest organizers and social networks that may support movement participation.

As a reminder, at the world-systemic level, social media spaces controlled by these corporations become the marketplace where the user's attention is bought and sold, and attention is the last "product" core countries like the United States are able to manipulate to maintain their global economic hegemony. Going beyond a material economy where tangible goods are exchanged, or even a knowledge economy where useful ideas and efficiency are sold, the U.S. economy today thrives on the attention economy, where little of tangible value to society is sold. Users are encouraged to be glued to their devices, looking at whatever each user's unique algorithm propels them toward. The information about where users look is then used to generate more profit within the attention economy. To put it simply, without manipulating people's attention online for profit, the U.S. empire would experience a serious threat to its hegemonic status. Thus U.S. interests in maintaining hegemonic status determines the boundaries of online discourse.

Discourse is unlikely to feature movements that seriously threaten the current capitalist world-system. When discourse does succeed in garnering attention toward such revolutionary movements, additional factors within the structures of social media play an active role in stifling their success, which is measured in *offline* protest participation. To demonstrate some of these patterns we can look at figure 4.3, which shows the number of participants who attended offline protests led by different identity groups across 141 countries over twenty-eight years. As the percent of people in the world who have access to the internet increased in the last three decades, certain kinds of protests experienced larger offline turnouts, whereas other kinds of protests experienced smaller offline turnouts. Most notably, protests led by anarchist identifying groups experienced significantly higher offline participation compared to other groups. In contrast, protests led by Black radical identifying groups experienced significantly lower offline participation across countries over the years as the percent of people using the internet increased.

Based on these patterns, we can infer that the attention economy possibly stifles social movements with clear and distinct *alternative imaginaries* that threaten the capitalist world-system.

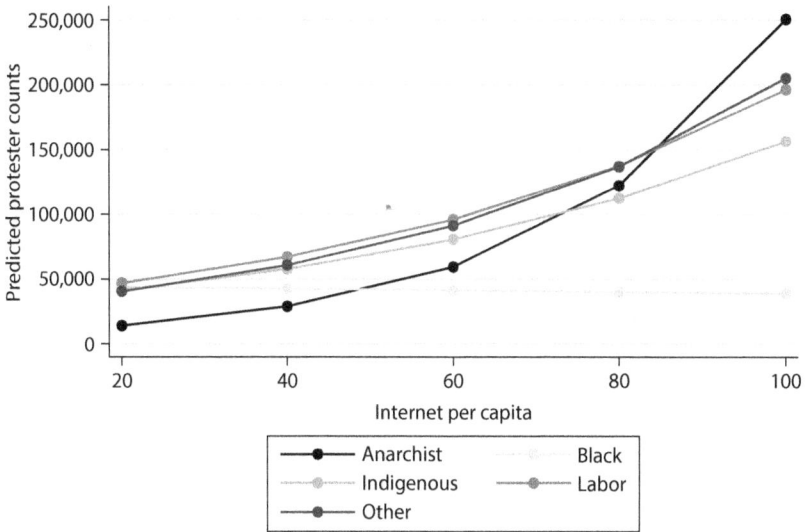

**FIGURE 4.3** Predicted count of protesters by identity * internet.

*Source*: Previously published in the *Journal of World Systems Research* and reproduced here under their open access polity and creative commons license.

"Anarchy" is not a clearly defined political category with a unified alternative imaginary to the capitalist world-system. Many anarchist groups are anarcho-capitalists and organize around antigovernment, pro-capital imaginaries. In recent years, enthusiasts of virtual cryptocurrency have gained a lot of attention for their political identification with anarchy.[35] As crypto-discourse has exploded in online culture over the last decade, these kinds of libertarian, pro-capitalist groups have gained tremendous support. Many anarchist groups are explicitly antigovernment and anticapitalist, but "anarchy" as an umbrella concept is not automatically a threat to the existing capitalist imaginary, and recent popular iterations of the identification are very much aligned with the neoliberal imaginary.

Black radical groups tend to historically organize against police brutality and state violence that is employed to maintain the capitalist world-system. These movements have distinct *alternative imaginaries* that center on the abolition of systems of policing and mass incarceration. These systems are critical in maintaining the capitalist economic structure of core states such as the hegemonic United States. As more people use the internet globally, movements that present the alternative imaginary of abolition see a decrease in offline protest participation. This may read as counterintuitive given the rise in the prominence of movements such as Black Lives Matter in online discourse. However, *visibility* in discourse does not automatically indicate successful mobilizations.

As social movement organizations become more sophisticated with the advancement of communication technologies, so does the power of *counter movements*. Counter movements can occur in seemingly innocuous ways, for example, when neoliberal ideals successfully penetrate revolutionary efforts. In his book *Revolution Without Revolutionaries: Making Sense of the Arab Spring*, the sociologist Asef Bayat coined the term "refolutions" (reformist revolutions) to describe movements that are revolutionary in their goals but neoliberal in their underlying ideologies.[36] Although the movements across the Middle East desired revolutionary outcomes, they primarily desired political changes without addressing capitalism. Bayat specifically highlights NGOs as institutions that penetrate activist spaces in a counterrevolutionary way because NGOs are predisposed to neoliberal ideals and fundamentally opposed to wealth distribution.

Neoliberal forces have similarly integrated into the Black Lives Matter movement. Although the movement is fundamentally abolitionist, it has also been appropriated by neoliberal institutions to engage in "woke-washing."[37] Consistent with Fisher's ideas in *Capitalist Realism*, corporations appropriate abolition to sell products and reproduce capitalism. A popular example of this phenomenon is the 2017 Pepsi ad featuring the elite celebrity Kendall Jenner participating in a Black Lives Matter protest in which the narrative ends with Jenner passing a Pepsi to a cop monitoring the protest.

Beyond these measures, ICTs and social media in particular enable—and perhaps encourage—another form of counter movement: minimal online activism, sometimes unkindly referred to in the literature as "slacktivism."[38] Continuing with the Black Lives Matter example, the hashtag #BlackLivesMatter or #BLM has been incredibly successful in raising awareness about police brutality through social media, and some scholars emphasize that the online movement supported massive riots and protests across all fifty states in the United States in 2020.[39] At the same time, other scholars highlight how the use of the hashtag far surpasses other forms of engagement with Black revolutionary movements.[40] In 2020, while massive numbers of people were on the streets, I remember that even larger numbers of people were protesting online with simple activities such as changing their profile pictures on Facebook and Instagram to black rectangles.

People could, of course, do both, and many people certainly did. But among the subsegment of the population that maintained its activist position to the profile picture, many surely felt they had contributed to the cause with such simple gestures. The more a movement is co-opted by neoliberal institutions, the easier it is to passively engage. When a movement is trending in the zeitgeist, most people in the discourse are motivated to engage; whether it's to gain social capital or get a sense of belonging, and people derive positive experiences from such engagement. When movements are not as in the zeitgeist, it becomes harder to feel the same effect from participation without a deeper engagement or even offline protest participation.

# 5

## MICRODOSING COLLECTIVE EFFERVESCENCE

Why are we online? What is the value of being online? What is the cost of not being online, and who bears that cost? Am I online because it makes me happy? What makes me happy? Do the same things that make me happy also make other people happy? Does what makes one happy depend on the context of one's life, which varies dramatically across people, places, cultures, and histories? Or does happiness transcend historical biographies and tap into something more fundamentally human—love, connection, belonging? If so, is suffering fundamental too—grief, disconnection, illness? What about unnatural suffering created by the way we decide to organize society—credit cards, prison cells, gender binaries? What about unnatural happiness—Amazon packages, mobile phones, picket fences? If natural suffering is loss, grief, and disconnection, then can natural happiness be anything but the direct opposite, i.e., belonging, love, and connection? What is *real*? If what is real is all that occurs naturally, then isn't everything else *constructed* and therefore *mutable*? Is offline society mutable? Is online society mutable? Does transforming online society change offline society? Does a key to collective happiness in our historical epoch hang in the balance between online and offline activity?

# ALIENATION

## Child Brides, Child Labor, and Immigrants

Only two generations ago my grandmother, Laxmi Devi Pokharel, grew up in Gulariya, a town in Bardia district in rural, far western Nepal. When she was seven years old, she was married to a feudal lord. Her family waited until she was one year older before sending her to live with her new husband. I don't know the man's name, and I guess I could ask my mom but I don't care to know. When Laxmi was twelve years old, her husband married a second wife and kept them both in separate houses across from each other. Laxmi got the older, dilapidated house. Laxmi was an exceptional human being. During the Nepali Civil War, all the feudal family homes in Gulariya were raided by Maoist insurgents, except Laxmi's house. She had a reputation for treating people kindly, especially people who were less privileged. Because the insurgents were oppressed members of the community, they had a respect for my grandmother that they did not have for any other ruling class member. My mother, Reeta Pokharel, was Laxmi's youngest child. Her marriage was arranged to my dad, Prakash Bhandari, when she was fifteen years old. Prakash was visiting the Bardia region from the capital Kathmandu and saw Reeta at a family friend's wedding and decided he would marry her. Prakash was from one of the most respected brahmin families in the country. His father, Dhundiraj Bhandari, was a great scholar and a historian in his time. Reeta's parents did not have to think twice before accepting the marriage proposal. My mom sometimes tells me that she slept in her own mother's arms right up until the day she was married and had to move across the country to Kathmandu. She was sent to Kathmandu with two paid domestic helpers from the Indigenous Tharu community in Bardia: Juni Tharu, age eleven, and Shyam Lal Tharu, age ten.

Reeta had to learn about elite city culture quickly to survive, and she spent all of her time attending to social affairs and building connections. She had my brother when she was nineteen, and me when she was twenty-two. Juni was our primary caregiver

*(continued on next page)*

(*continued from previous page*)

> while my mom tried to carve herself a space in this strange new world. Juni and Shyam eventually fell in love and married. I spent a lot of my early years with Juni and my paternal grandpa (the historian) who was my best friend. When I was seven, my grandpa died from colon cancer. His treatments cost my parents everything, so when I was eight, both my parents moved to the United States to find work and support us financially. My brother and I lived with Juni, Shyam, and their son Suhel for two years when I was eight and nine. They are my family as much as my parents are, yet they are my parents' employees who joined our family as child laborers.
>
> My mom returned from the United States when I was ten, but my dad remained in the United States, working at a gas station in Maryland seven days a week for below minimum wage. I moved to the United States for college when I was eighteen. In my junior year of college returned to Nepal, after a decade of working menial jobs in the United States.
>
> Much later in life my dad told me that after September 11 he had to leave everything behind and move across the country because of the dramatic rise in hate crimes against brown folks. A friend of his had been murdered by an angry mob, and my dad was constantly subjected to physical and verbal attacks. Back in Nepal the Brahmanical Hindu society that my dad and I hail from detests Muslims with an equally fiery passion. Recently one of my cousins converted to Islam, and he was ostracized from the family community and had to migrate to a different part of the country. He got fired from his job as a respected schoolteacher in Gulariya. Nobody has heard from him since.

Laying out the story of my heritage in this way is woefully tragic because I must reckon with my own privilege relative not only to the children my family employed but also to my own parents, *even my father who embodies the very concept of privilege from most lenses.* In my time living in the United States as a woman of color, I have experienced plenty of microaggressions (and a few macroaggressions), but nothing ever came close to the assault one could face for appearing to be a brown person and possibly Muslim in 2001.

The most oppressed I have felt in my life was when my parents had to leave me to earn money, and I was too small to be left behind. Reflecting on that now, I can't help but feel guilty for feeling oppressed in that context because Juni-*didi* and Shaym-*dai* were only slightly older when *they* had to leave their families to earn money. They were subjected to the most hellish version of my worst emotional experience simply because they were poor, Tharu, and at the bottom of the caste hierarchy. Their own son Suhel was only one year old when Juni-*didi* and Shyam-*dai* became fully responsible for me and my brother, taking care of three children on an extremely limited budget. My parents would have been able to send only small remittances from their work for below minimum wage. We were never quite food insecure, but there was only just enough for our family of five, nothing extra, no eating out, no splurging on candy or on frivolous things. We got one pair of new clothes for Dashain, and that was it. Nobody—neither my parents nor Juni-*didi*—will give me a straight answer when I ask now how they were compensated during this period of financial struggle. It's a thought loop that leads me to a dark place, but I do know that today my Tharu-employee-family are proud homeowners in Kathmandu, a major global city. Juni-*didi* and Shyam-*dai*'s success story is *the* neoliberal fantasy. They had "worked hard" since they were small children, and now they have access to material and social power that their own ancestors could never dream of having. *It only cost them their entire childhoods.*

Capitalism is an economic system that cannot exist without stealing people—and specifically children—away from their loved ones. Human disconnection is a necessary condition for unfettered capital accumulation. If all people spent their days laughing with their grandparents and playing with their children, who would supply the labor necessary to accumulate capital?

Returning to where this book began, in *Capital* Marx consistently makes the case that capital cannot exist without exploiting labor-power. Per the labor theory of value, surplus value is only possible to extract from labor-power and labor-time. Labor is the natural, human, *real* face of the conceptual, abstracted, *constructed* capital.[1] Capital only exists as a theoretical potential that is realized through the manifest experience of human labor.[2]

What happens when there is a surplus of *potential* capital but there are not enough people to provide the labor required to support its manifestation? Surprisingly, this question leads me to Babasaheb Ambedkar's explanation of the phenomenon of child brides in brahmin society. In *Castes in India: Their Mechanism, Genesis and Development*, Ambedkar explains that child brides became common in brahmin society due to the problem of the "surplus man."[3] For brahmins to maintain their status quo in Hindu society, they had to enforce rules of endogamy. This would ensure that folks from outside the brahmin community could not become a part of the enclosed group by marrying into the top of the caste hierarchy. For this scheme to work, however, there needed to be a demographic balance of traditionally marriageable genders—i.e., men and women—of marriageable age. In practice, this was never the case due to many factors, including the deaths of spouses. These situations would lead to the problem of a "surplus man" who could theoretically marry outside of the brahmin caste and bring the whole enclosed class project crashing down. Their thinking on the "surplus woman" (i.e., widows) was that she could simply be forced to jump into her late husband's funeral pyre and kill herself. Since such a fate was unimaginable for the "surplus man," the brahmins would have to expand the definition of "marriageable" to include children. This way, all widowers would be able to find brides from within the brahmin caste.

In a similar way, when there is a surplus of potential capital and not enough labor, children provide the labor-power needed to keep the bourgeoise at the top of the class hierarchy. Brahmanism and capitalism intersect at their foundational necessity for the suffering of marginalized groups and children. In other words, these two ruling classes intersect at the nexus of extreme trauma and suffering that is imposed on vulnerable populations before they enter adulthood and often even adolescence.

## ALIENATION 2.0

The attention economy relies on this age-old formula: suffering of marginalized groups + exploitation of children = manifest power at the top of the hierarchy. This dynamic is most visible in how the Marxist concept of *alienation* transmutes into its most sinister form in the attention economy. The reality we navigate today is far from the forgone historical materialist conclusions that the alienation of labor—i.e., the real humans producing abstract capital—would lead to a proletarian revolution and the end of capitalism. The attention economy innovates instead by turning alienation into capital in such a way that capital manifested through this particular economy is inseparable from alienation. Alienation is capital, capital is alienation. In the online economy of attention, capital only exists as a theoretical potential that is realized through the manifest experience of human alienation.

Marx coined the concept of alienation specifically in the context of factory work in the factory system. Factory workers are alienated because they must separate their intellectual abilities from their labor functions.[4] Early capitalists separated creativity from work with the explicit purpose of diminishing labor to physical activity. The first time I heard about this concept was in my Sociology 101 class in the first semester of college. My mentor, Liz Cherry, explained Marxist alienation in what remains the simplest and clearest way to describe this concept to a broader audience. She described the production process for the aglet—the small plastic or metal sheath attached at the end of shoelaces and drawstrings. At factories now predominantly located across the developing world, there are workers of all ages whose entire job day in and day out is to attach the aglet to a drawstring ten hours a day, six days a week. Other workers would be responsible for weaving the shoelace into the sneakers ten hours a day, six days a week. Before modern capitalism, cobblers would engage creative and intellectual labor to first design a shoe in their mind and then put together the whole product.

This purposeful endeavor is how Marx states we are different from animals: we don't act physically and instinctively to create; our creation is intentional, and this intentionality is the key characteristic that makes our species human beings. In the factories, the ruling class purposefully removes this fundamental humanity from the workforce, so it can monopolize intellectual and creative work. The labor force, meanwhile, is reduced to a machine, and their humanity dies in the process of tacking on aglet after aglet. Their functions are kept separate from the shoelace weaver, so they cannot talk to other laborers about their lifelessness. They lose sense of their species-being. They are alienated from themselves, their work, and other people. They are reduced to capital-generating machines.

Some readings of Marxist theory suggest that alienation is what leads to the end of capitalism by way of authoritarian socialism and, ultimately, utopian communism.[5] The alienated workers eventually come together in their shared struggle as an oppressed proletariat class and wage revolutionary war against the ruling bourgeoise class. In this reading, Marx's views on technology within this description of historical development is deeply optimistic. In *Karl Marx on Technology and Alienation*, Amy Wendling describes how Marx sees the role of technology:

> Marx cites the *Communist Manifesto* in chapter XV of *Capital* in order to show how the constant revolutionizing of the means of production in the capitalist period not only marks a journey through purgatory, but is also a positive accumulation of scientific resources. Just as purgatory is a necessity for ascension to heaven, the season in the capitalist inferno is a historical necessity because it lays the foundation for the communist mode of production. Alienated labor is the purgation. In its wake, it puts down a surplus objectification of human labor, heralding the new economic era. This surplus is returned when the mode of production is changed from capitalism to communism.[6]

In this reading of Marx, the way he engages with technological development is inseparable from his predictions about the end of capitalism. The alienation of labor is a necessary evil until a time when technological and mechanical advancement drastically reduces the need for human labor. In these calculations, the timeline aligns marvelously so that when the alienated workforce has had just enough of capitalist oppression, science and technology will have advanced enough to support a communistic way of life.

In envisioning technological advancement as necessary for social progress, Marx clearly could not have imagined modern online life under late capitalism. When I say "late" capitalism, this is not coming from a place of utopian Marxism but from an acknowledgment of the aggressive environmental impacts of capitalism—as well how it signals the possible end of the human race and any economic systems we may have constructed in our time here. The arbiters of the attention economic system are certainly responding to this element of the lateness of capitalism. They have innovated beyond the Earth's natural limitations in a way that Marx could not have anticipated. In its current iteration, this particular technology is less a purgatory of alienation and more like straight up hell.

The fundamental innovation in how we create surplus value for the ruling class in the attention economic system is this: unlike the factory owner, the app-owner knows that no aspect of the human animal should be wasted in the pursuit of capital. The attention economy has tapped into the previously untapped potential of converting the bodies *and* minds of the population into capital.[7] Machines can now easily tack an aglet onto any shoe much faster than a person ever could, so the best remaining way to extract capital from people is to give them their creative faculties back and convert every thought and idea they ever had into capital.

The alienation we face in the attention economic system is not because we are separated from our creative potential but because we are pushed to constantly *exhaust* our creative potential. The alienation we face in the attention economic system is not because we are separated from other people but because we are constantly exposed to other people and pitted against each other in a two-dimensional imitation of society. Everything about how alienation operates in this late capitalist economy is counterintuitive to the Marxist concept, *yet the outcome at the level of our humanity remains the same.* The constant urge to create content, like, comment, share with the hopes of finding social approval often leads to a similar sense of disconnection as that experienced by a worker in the factory system. However, this feeling is now *productive* in a way factory alienation could not have been. This feeling generates surplus value for the ruling class. This feeling is now capital. Absolutely no part of the human animal is left unmonetized in late capitalism. This incredibly productive cycle cannot continue without sufficient bodies and minds to exploit, and because capital needs to grow indefinitely, the ruling class needs to continually expand the total global population that is online. Development projects such as ICT4D that aim to expand ICT access across the globe align neatly with ruling class interests.

*When the ruling class runs out of minds to exploit, they exploit children for capital.* The reality is that we are living through multiple global pandemics. Society has decided to collectively ignore the crippling and debilitating addiction young people and children have developed to ICTs.[8] The ruling class ruthlessly exploits and alienates children to accumulate capital. This formula always works. Of course, the most vulnerable children who perform the most productive mental labor for the attention economy are at the bottom of the socioeconomic hierarchy. In one study of middle-school-aged children, Feng, Ma, and Zhong found that "social anxiety partially mediates the impact of stress on internet addiction and social class indirectly influences internet addiction by moderating the relationship between stress and social anxiety."[9] In other words, *children from the poorest backgrounds experience the highest levels of stress, and they cope with this stress by developing a dependence on the internet for the social validation they don't receive offline.*

Many children turn to the internet to feel better about the material inequality they experience in the real world, but their oppression is further exploited by turning their need for belonging into dependence and their dependence into capital.

By the time most kids—especially kids from lower socioeconomic backgrounds—reach adulthood in late capitalism, they have become seamlessly integrated into the productive forces of the attention economy, and they have become deeply alienated. The less advantaged they are in offline society, the more likely they are to become alienated online. Their childhoods are lost staring at screens and performing labor for tech billionaires, all with the hope of finding connection and belonging.

## ATTENTION

### The Chosen One

One evening nearly a year after my grandfather died and both my parents left for the United States, I was hanging out alone on the veranda of our family home in Old Baneshwor Height and felt the warmth of tears in my eyes. Finally, to my relief, I was able to cry about my grandpa's death. Until then I had been convinced that something was deeply wrong with me because my best friend had died and I could not cry. I was certainly not incapable of feelings. When my mom left the country (and then my dad a month later), I had no trouble breaking down, screaming, crying, limbs flailing at the airport with everyone watching.

But when *buwa* (grandpa) died, I was just . . . curious. Where did he go, exactly? What is this whole death business? The night before he died, I had been to the hospital to visit him. When it was just the two of us, he said "this is our last meeting" and some other stuff. I can't remember the other stuff, even after many years and many different kinds of therapy. I suppose the "last meeting" part was significant enough to drown out the rest, but it feels like such a loss to be unable to access his parting wisdom. Until then I had spent all my time receiving wisdom from this verifiably great scholar. An epitome of brahmin excellence, the priestliest of scholars, a wellspring of knowledge, God's chosen one. *Buwa* was living evidence to the brahmin community that they deserved their status in society. He was kind, a vegetarian, and humble.

Most of my early childhood was spent listening to *buwa* tell me Hindu and Buddhist stories about wisdom, grace, and the triumph of good over evil. My favorite story was about Prince Siddhartha Gautam (of Lumbini, near my own birthplace of Siddharthangar) and his triumph over human suffering. Buwa must have told me that story hundreds of times, and it was never enough. I would drive him up a wall asking him to repeat the story, and he always yielded with kindness and patience. After he died, I never heard that story again. I never heard any more stories until I started reading and writing them myself when the computer came to my house. *Buwa* supposedly told everyone who would listen that I would become a "*bidushi*" (wise female scholar) someday.

Here I am, living out my priestly legacy. The seeds for my future were planted in my soul by God's absolute and verified favorite, and failure was not in the prophecy. If Laxmi Devi Pokharel's family had not connected with Dhundiraj Bhandari's family through my mother's child marriage, my own future would likely have gone in the direction of child marriage. Instead, that day on the veranda my eight-year-old self decided to sit down cross-legged, teary-eyed, and talk directly with the stars about the possibility of a very different kind of future.

Many of the people I encounter in my life as a scholar in the United States, even at an elite college, have never heard of Nepal. Most people I meet assume I am Indian. Those who have heard of Nepal usually know my country in stereotypes: "Did you go to Mount Everest all the time?" "The weed in Kathmandu must be next level." "Something about yoga and meditation." I have repeated many variations of "It's nearly impossible to get to Everest base camp without significant physical training." "The weed in Kathmandu is terrible." and "Did you know Buddha was born in Nepal?"

Truthfully, I would rather answer these same three or four questions about Nepal repeatedly than be presumed Indian.

The stereotypes at least validate my national and cultural identity; they make me feel like a real person from a real place. When people think I am Indian, my existence is reduced to the singular aspect of skin color, erasing the complex power dynamics between my nation and theirs that are produced by India's local hegemonic status. Conversely, I love it when people associate Nepal with the Buddha and want to talk to me about meditation. I rarely practice yoga, but meditation is a core element of my personal identity. My practice spontaneously started on that veranda that evening when I was a small child, and in many ways it feels like my whole life has been moving toward formalizing that commitment to being still and going inward.

## THE ANATOMY OF ATTENTION

My interest in the phenomenon of *attention* is a natural outcome of my lifelong journey inward. Meditation is the practice of sharpening the quality of our attention. Most practitioners can agree on that definition across differences in national, cultural, and spiritual boundaries. Anyone who practices meditation seriously—from Hindu gurus and Buddhist monks in Nepal to the rapidly expanding population of secular practitioners in the West—understands the value of attention.[10] Some even argue that our attention is the most valuable naturally occurring— "real"—resource we have access to in human existence.[11] There are both religious and scientific explanations for this value. On the religious/spiritual side, some traditions believe that what we pay attention to constructs our whole experience of reality. There is no such thing as time: past or present. The present moment is all that exists. The entirety of existence is nothing but choices about where we focus our attention from one present moment to another. Some traditions hold the belief that all phenomena are causally interdependent: whatever we manifest in the next present moment is predicated upon what we chose to pay attention to in the preceding moment.[12] Spiritually, attention is all there is to experience. Nothing that is real is more powerful than attention. Attention leads us to God. Attention *is* God.

On the more tempered scientific side, scholars emphasize the measurable outcomes of improved quality of attention.[13] Some empirically validated benefits of reclaiming our attention include decreased stress and increased productivity.[14] In *The Mindful Elite: Mobilizing from the Inside Out*, the sociologist Jaime Kucinskas describes the secularization and subsequent popularity of meditation techniques across major U.S. institutions as an elite-led social movement.[15] The movement to popularize meditation as a science-backed, secular practice with measurable health benefits began with Jon Kabat-Zinn's Mindfulness-Based Stress Reduction (MBSR) program at the University of Massachusetts Medical Center in the late 1970s. Kucinskas walks us through the last forty or more years of the movement that purposefully rebranded a religious, Buddhist practice to appeal to mainstream American audiences. Consequently, today mindfulness is a staple health initiative at corporate headquarters, hospitals, schools, and colleges. The leaders of this movement picked and chose aspects of traditional Buddhist practices that could be measured (for example, self-reported levels of happiness or efficiency) and applied rhetoric specifically appealing to different institutions with the explicit intent of acquiring mainstream acceptance for this previously stigmatized practice. The leaders of these movements held elite positions across key secular institutions, which gave them access to these spaces.

In her interview with the leaders of this movement, Kucinskas uncovered how this movement started with specific anticapitalist and anticonsumerist intentions, which are values embedded within the principles of many Buddhist schools of thought. In the process of rebranding for different institutions, especially corporations, specific spiritual and religious elements that promoted anticapitalist values became lost. The results of this form of secularized mainstream acceptance of mindfulness are truly ironic. Today capitalists promote meditation to meet the goals of increasing labor efficiency and "mindfulness" is a massive profit-generating industry.

These practices are especially prominent within the corporate culture of Silicon Valley: the ruling class in the attention economic system. Every year Silicon Valley leaders host the Wisdom 2.0 conference in the San Francisco Bay area to discuss the benefits of meditation, while simultaneously building massive amounts of wealth from buying and selling our attention.[16]

Capital, it turns out, is more powerful than God.

The *real*, naturally occurring, endlessly powerful resource of attention converts into the construct of *capital* on the internet. Before the internet—perhaps more specifically smartphones and *mobile* internet that follow us wherever we go—it would be an unending task to envision a technology that could so seamlessly convert attention into capital. Back in the days of cable, we could just change the channel during commercials. Today we are the channel.

In some ways, I wish we could go back and delete, delete, delete. There are days and weeks and months when everything feels entirely hopeless. The planet is on its last legs. Poverty and destitution are expansive. Everywhere I direct my attention, I see genocides, hate, brahminism, racism, sexism, homophobia, transphobia, and ableism. Nobody in America has health care, and the white rural working class blames the immigrants while pharmaceutical corporations earn record profits from a historic global pandemic. Our government sends billions of our dollars seemingly every week to support a brutal livestream genocide in the Middle East, as we mindlessly scroll past violent images featuring mass deaths of small children to redirect our limited attention to clips from an Eras Tour we cannot afford to attend in person.

We walk to cafés that support the genocide we want to look away from – the café that also starves Mexican farmers – wearing sneakers made by ten-year-old factory workers in Bangladesh and log right back on to Twitter—which is now called X because a ruling elite decided he wants to *own discourse*—and we throw stones at two-dimensional imitations of human beings because our favorite celebrity popstar that we put on a pedestal is dating a loose-lipped person who seems like a racist. For that fleeting moment, we get to feel like we are not a part of the problem because someone else is. Better yet, we get to feel like we are a part of the solution because we have taken time out of our long day slaving away at the gig economy to educate some unknowable entity on the internet. We are better than fans of *that* band! Either there will be 0.000001 percent less racism in the world because of our contribution, or at least every two-dimensional onlooker will know that the tiny construct of space our own imitation occupies represents a *good* three-dimensional person.

I've been in every iteration of this painfully familiar online interaction. Wanting to feel like a good person is so quintessentially human. My meditations have taught me that I need to release this attachment to my image. It's a work in progress.

The truth is that it's impossible to be good in the way that I want to be. I am a bad ally. It's in my DNA. Buwa was a lovely grandfather and perhaps a decent scholar but was also a terrible imprint on Nepali caste society. He literally imported my teenage mom and two children from an oppressed community to serve as wife and domestic help in his home. That is without accounting for the various structural traumas brahmin men like him have imposed upon the entire fabric of my country. I cannot erase this element of my history no matter how badly I feel about the crimes against humanity committed by my ancestry. There was a time when I would awkwardly tell people, "well, I am not actually brahmin because I am not Hindu anymore. I'm Buddhi-flexible," citing my passionate support of Amebdkar's Navayana Buddhism and *The Dalit Buddhist Movement*.[17] By renouncing Hinduism, I hoped I could erase the brahmin from my identity. When I married my white American husband, I found myself in the funniest little dilemma. I had an opportunity to give up my brahmin name *Bhandari* and take on my husband's name McElrath. Either I would be a bad ally to oppressed castes, or I would be a bad feminist. I kept my name. Accepting that I am a bad ally is a sincere acknowledgment of the reality that my brahmanism and all the privileges it awards me will accompany me to my grave. Feeling bad about that is a narcissistic instinct to refocus on myself as the victim of a system that heralded me here to a platform few people in this world have.

There is no threshold of self-flagellation I can reach where I stop becoming complicit in the systemic injustices of Nepali brahmin society. That instinct to feel badly about our complicity in the construction of suffering is purely egoic. So often I witness this "main character syndrome" in dominant caste Hindus in Nepal and white liberals in the United States. I've been there, and I understand the impulse. Although, on the level of praxis, what does the self-flagellation accomplish? It quite literally creates more suffering.

Can we eradicate the suffering of others with our own suffering? Or can we perhaps choose *not* to suffer while emphasizing the suffering of those systemically harmed? Can we listen and learn their visions of the future without taking the past so *personally* all the time?

If a lifelong obsession with suffering has taught me one thing, it is that I am completely useless when I am suffering. When I feel really, existentially bad, I am incapable of performing everyday tasks such as taking a shower, let alone more complex tasks of leading a classroom discussion about caste and capitalism. Losing the ability to be present for my students with energy, passion, and enthusiasm is harmful to them. Not being able to love my toddler son Neel in every way that he deserves is harmful to him. Whether it's through teaching or parenting or activism or community engagement, the possibility of contributing to positive social change hinges on our personal well-being. If we want to create a world without unnatural suffering, we cannot start from a place of unnaturally suffering ourselves. It does not make any sense to try to clean the chimney using a bucket of soot.

As a teacher and a mother, I am accountable to my students and to my son. Inside the classroom I aim to create a transformative space honoring bell hooks's wisdom in *Teaching to Transgress*.[18] In this small space that I lead, everyone has a voice, and people who have been subjected to the most historical injustices have the loudest voices. My students learn from me, and I learn from them. Outside the classroom, students come to me during office hours with all kinds of struggles. I listen. I try to help in the ways I can. Some of what they share is devastating. Without a strong foundation of personal well-being, it would become very easy to disintegrate over their struggles and close my office door. That would be tragic. Sometimes I am *all* they have. This generation of people—who are coming upon adulthood in a world that promises them no real future in any sense of the word—are some of the kindest and most thoughtful human beings. They need me at my best so they can unpack their own suffering in my presence.

How we feel has a direct impact on the people we serve. Even though the attention economy is designed to make us feel this way, *most of us are not really, truly alone.* We are accountable to someone, somewhere. *Prioritizing our own well-being not for personal glory but as a service to others is instrumental to creating change. Healing is praxis.* Scholars of marginalized races and genders have repeated this truth over decades, most notably the intersectional feminist icon bell hooks, who centers healing and joy in her messaging about feminism, race, and pedagogy.[19]

When it comes to challenging the attention economic system, this critical messaging takes on a very literal shape. *Because a pervasive kind of alienation is required to socially reproduce the attention economy, healing by way of reclaiming authority over one's own attention is an overt act of resistance.*

So I choose to focus my valuable attention on different narratives about my journey that are also true. These narratives are less harsh and more triumphant. A Nepali woman from a lineage of child brides finds intellectual and academic success at a prestigious college in the richest country in the world. This journey should not have been possible. I am so lucky. I am going to use this gift to ease more of the suffering in the world through teaching, writing and community action. That is what my grandmother Laxmi Devi would have done had she found the same opportunities. *This* is my ancestral destiny.

Gratitude is my most sincere—and least defeatist—acknowledgment of the suffering of others. Yet there will always be a part of me that knows luck was only part of the story, the other part being my grandfather's legacy. I feel the *freest* when I stop trying to cover up the ancestral crimes of my family with ancestral traumas. Both exist, both are true elements of my construction. And it's *okay.* It's not my fault, per say. I'm not a "good person"

because of my traumas or a "bad person" because of the powers I inherited. I'm just an experience in a moment in space and
time, trying my best to improve the quality of this experience for
myself and others. I don't always get it right, and I sometimes get
it terribly wrong. That's okay too. If we are never wrong, we lose
the opportunity to grow and learn new ways of perception.

A massive problem we face today is that *nobody on the internet
is ever wrong, and the more singularly and unfailingly right people
on the internet are, the more surplus value they create for the attention economy.*

In Web 2.0 we are all reduced to poor imitations of our worst
impulses, and our deepest fears have become capitalized. Tony
Sampson's work on emotional contagion in the online social
network demonstrates that our fears quite literally translate to
capital in the attention economy. In *Virality: Contagion Theory
in the Age of Networks*, Sampson outlines how strong affects such
as fear and love are contagious in social media networks.[20] In
memetic analyses, we can see this process occurring, for example,
in how antivaccination rhetoric uses the fear of vaccines to build
massive online networks of support. Sampson also discusses how
empathy and love spread similarly and achieve virality online,
citing the 2008 election of Barack Obama as an example of
"positive contagion." We have lived through an entire decade
of Web 2.0 since Sampson's writing, and cyberutopian visions
of such positive contagion are more difficult to imagine. There
are fewer and fewer examples similar to the Occupy Movement
and Arab Spring today, and more and more examples such as
the antivax movement and climate change denialism. Sampson
envisioned the viral social network as a balance between polar-
izing but powerful emotions, but *in Web 2.0 fear is triumphant.*
Fear is a much better tool to ensure we keep creating, clicking,
and liking.

In a world where fear creates the most capital, healing is praxis. Healing is praxis because how we feel affects the people we serve in physical spaces that we occupy. Additionally, healing is praxis in this very specific way in the virtual spaces we occupy. *The first step to healing is acknowledging we have a problem. We are a society that is terribly addicted.* My students often tell me stories about how they picked up their phones with the intention of calling their parents, and three hours later they find themselves exhausted from reading about how the world is ending in seventeen different ways. The phone call often does not happen. Just like chemical substances, the attention economy has mind-altering effects that separate us from our intentions. Just like substances, the attention economy also alters our emotional state. We may start out happy, but often once we pick up our phones, we end up afraid. As with substances, the opposite is also true. Sometimes we feel completely unwell, and our phone provides the dopamine, escapism, and temporary relief we need to fill the void. In the long run, however, we need more and more dopamine to feel the same relief. This entire experience is now monetized by tech companies.

Our addiction and our children's addictions are critical for the ruling class in the attention economy to continue accumulating capital. They have colonized our attention: the most powerful resource available to us. It is absolutely critical to resist this colonization and heal from this addiction if we want real, lasting social change. Pushing this same technology, this toxic economy, on marginalized populations is a counterintuitive approach to progress. It is not our job to save people who don't have mobile internet. That mindset is nothing but an imperialist hangover. It is not our job to save anyone but ourselves. Saving ourselves is not possible without fundamentally altering our relationship with information and communication technologies. *Saving ourselves is not possible without reclaiming our attention.*

## TRANSFORMATION

### Healing Cycles, Hateful Seeds

I met Kevin in graduate school. We were part of the same friend group and bonded immediately upon meeting each other on the first day. We were close friends for two years before we dated and soon enough I was squarely and fully in the spiritual opposite of a child marriage. And that's what it took, honestly. The sense of belonging and triumphant agency.

It was only after this point that I truly began working on my mental health and well-being. My whole life before this, I had been searching for meaning but never actually noting what I found. I realized I had not been particularly scientific about addressing my own suffering. So, I tried some new methods backed by empirical data. I wrote gratitude journals; I ran a half-marathon and formalized my meditation practice. I began healing, and I continue to heal as I raise my toddler son with a wonderful human being in an **equal** partnership, *breaking cycles of generational trauma among the women in my lineage.*

*Still,* there is suffering everywhere, all around. Still, there is the voice in my head that knows that healing is only accessible to me because I am the granddaughter of the "chosen one" in a structure where those not deemed so chosen are subjected to systematic abuse, violence, and death. I honor the truth of my dual legacy in every moment. I recognize both truths, and I become the vessel that contains them without becoming identified with either.

# OTHER WELLNESS HACKS
# OF SILICON VALLEY

I have titled this chapter "microdosing collective effervescence," and that needs a little bit of unpacking. The phenomenon of "microdosing" psychedelic drugs such as LSD and psilocybin has gained popularity in Silicon Valley in recent years.[21] The culture of work in the attention economy emphasizes "hacking" wellness, as is evident through, for example, the mainstreaming of meditation and MBSR in corporate headquarters for Google and Apple. Well, meditation takes a lot of effort, commitment, and most importantly time. Neoliberal capitalist economies depend on short-term-profit-engineering to the cost of everything else, including a habitable planet. Is a hack that doesn't work immediately to increase employee productivity even a hack? Enter the microdosing culture.

Stemming from the psychedelic renaissance, microdosing touts the same mental health benefits as good old macrodosing, without similarly robust scientific data backing up these claims.[22] Microdosing also does not require the same level of preparation, therapeutic hours, and integration as macrodosing. A single perceptual dose of psilosybin and LSD in a therapeutic setting is strongly correlated with several mental health benefits, including the treatment of depression, anxiety, and addiction.[23] Although it is a lot more "efficient" than meditation, this kind of therapy requires a lot of commitment to real, deep healing. A deeply healed workforce may begin to wonder, potentially, why they are designing apps that track people's every hope, dream, and fear. What if the workers could access the efficiency provided by mindfulness or therapeutic psychedelics without a threatening level of healing? What if it became trendy to take *subperceptual* doses of psychedelic drugs at work every day? That is essentially what microdosing culture offers: the most beneficial wellness "hack" for corporations.

Unlike with therapeutic macrodosing—colloquially, "tripping"—there are few or no studies done to indicate that microdosing is safe. Some of the stated benefits of therapeutic tripping is that a single session can create lasting and positive changes in the moods of patients with PTSD or provide long-term relief from addiction and chemical dependence.[24] Microdosing, however, *is chemical dependence.* There are no studies to show that psychedelic drugs are chemically addictive at subperceptual doses—largely because there are *no proper studies on microdosing*—but if you need to take a drug to feel good every day, then your well-being is dependent on that drug. The same logic applies to psychopharmacological medicines such as antidepressants, but unlike daily microdoses of LSD, those drugs have undergone rigorous safety tests. Nonetheless, the reality is that people who rely on those medications are dependent (albeit mostly safely) on those medications to feel good every day.

In *Radical Happiness: Moments of Collective Joy*, Lynne Segal addresses the tensions between psychopharmacological drugs and collective effervescence.[25] Collective effervescence is a concept coined by sociologist Émile Durkheim to describe a feeling of collective, other-worldly emotional exaltation that comes from sharing rituals with large crowds.[26] Though Durkheim's concept was developed in the context of religious ceremonies, over the years scholars have used these definitions to explain exalted states of collective emotions is spaces like protests and concerts.[27] (In my only successful experience with the elusive problem of virality, I once wrote an article about how pop singer Taylor Swift's Era's Tour concert provides contemporary examples of collective effervescence.)[28]

In Segal's book, she argues that the massive increase in mental illness in recent decades is symptomatic of a collective dissatisfaction with life under capitalism. Yet capitalism tries to solve the problem it created by mining for more capital. The pharmaceutical industrial complex makes record profits every year from severely overprescribing medicines such as selective serotonin reuptake inhibitors (SSRIs), which usually require a lifetime of drug purchases.[29] Some people really benefit from these medications, but others don't benefit at all and some experience harm.[30]

Many people are prescribed higher and higher doses of these drugs when they don't work. Meanwhile, patients continue to feel deeply unwell because the source of their disease is socio-economic even if the manifestation is chemical.[31]

In the same vein, Segal argues that *true* happiness and joy are collective in nature. In a protest march, at a rally, at the rooftop of Baneshwor Height in 2006, in Tahrir Square in Cairo in 2011, in Shaheen Bagh in Delhi in 2019, and in Black Lives Matter Plaza in Seattle in 2020, we find moments of collective joy. In those moments, we become a part of something much bigger than ourselves. The happiness we feel is limitless. It's not individualistic, it's not egoic, it's really not about the *me* in any way, it's about *us*. The more we share this kind of happiness, the more it grows. There is no better expression of joy. Most people desire such joy, such a complete sense of belonging to something greater than themselves.

The darker and more sinister our alienation gets, the more we dream of rising up together and fighting back. Unfortunately, we are exhausted, and they have all the money and the weapons and the militia and power. We fall deeper and deeper into our despair while they convert every ounce of our alienation into capital. But we don't stop seeking, we can't stop seeking— seeking is fundamental to our humanity. So we microdose that feeling of collective joy every day on the Web 2.0 imitation of life. We do so by liking the right likes and sharing the right shares and pushing to belong. This "slacktivism" is our attempt to address the deep feelings of dread and despair so characteristic of online life in late capitalism. However, similar to microdosing with psychedelics, microdosing collective effervescence does not support real healing and possibly creates more dependence and addiction, often by socially reproducing the attention economic system.

## DREAMS OF TRANSFORMATION
## AND JUSTICE

Slacktivism is far from the biggest issue with online social movements. I have discussed my hesitancy to use this word in this book and in other writing. Slacktivism implies a lack of caring, which is not often what people experience when they engage in these movements. Let's unpack it a little bit. What constitutes an online social movement activity? How do we define certain patterns of likes, clicks, and shares as social movement participation? The boundaries are blurry, and online social movement participation eludes strict definition.

My instinct is to believe that most people who use social media have done some kind of posting—or liking or sharing—that supports some kind of social or political agenda. The level of activity varies greatly from person to person, of course. There is a notable difference between, for example, linking a post that uses hashtag #Blacklivesmatter on X versus sharing tactics to evade cops during an ongoing riot on a decentralized direct messaging platform such as Signal. To reiterate with a slightly different kind of example, there is a notable difference between upvoting a post that raises concerns about giving an infant the COVID-19 vaccine due to the lack of long-term data on the subreddit r/Parents, versus creating a post that outlines how the government invented COVID-19 vaccines to implant microchip trackers to control the population on the subreddit r/Conspiracy.

Those are all examples of "online social movement activity," but they outline completely different behaviors with separate motivations, levels of engagement, passion, and commitment. Underlying all this activity is a common dissatisfaction with modern existence, an ennui corresponding to the most sinister forms of alienation. As we produce capital for the attention economy, we try to tend to our wounds in the same space where they are created, *because that's where everyone else seems to be.*

In the process of searching for community, many people end up more isolated. The search for belonging and lasting happiness gets more desperate as people align themselves with different Web 2.0 communities to meet their fundamental needs for connection. Every online community creates a unique social orbit, and the orbit comes with unique norms, rules of conduct, beliefs, ideologies, and values that are nonnegotiable yet foreign to nonmembers. Users subscribe to the rules of conduct of their respective groups because that makes them feel they are part of something bigger than themselves. But when they encounter people from other orbits with different, even opposing sets of rules, then society breaks down. This happens over and over again.

Society is constantly breaking down on the internet.

Public internet spaces such as X and Instagram are the point of intersection of different universes with different perceptual experiences of reality, based on different sets of rules and a different definition of "truth." Of course, some of these subjective truths are objectively true, in the sense that we can use Western enlightenment scientific methods to empirically validate that this version of reality is experienced materially and resolutely by collective society. Part of the problem, however, is that the premise of these objective truths have also been questioned, and questioning the authority of the scientific method is an infallible rule of belonging in certain orbits. We can see this, for example, in the myriad online communities committed to conspiracy theories, most visibly groups opposed to vaccinations. Although vaccine opposition fails to meet the standard for credibility by most orbits that subscribe to rationality as a core identity, there are forms of subjectivity that are reasonably accommodated by the same orbits to some degree. For example, subaltern critiques of Western empirical methods may similarly resist the notion of objectivity because of the imperialist biases embedded within the design of such methodology.[32] Even I engage such critiques in this book as an argument in favor of combining Western empirical data with my own experiences to fully describe the political economy of the internet.

The point is, the discourse encompasses many ways—both credible and otherwise—in which the notion of objectivity is a matter of debate. Each orbit subscribes to a different view on objectivity, so what we have in the social field is fragments of possibilities. It is in this decidedly postmodern reality that "online culture" is created and recreated, and in that culture everyone is looking for home. *But it is unclear how to find home, exactly.* Every orbit splits into multiple other orbits because so many versions of truths are constantly being created. At any moment, you are liable to break the rules; and the moment the rules are broken, you risk ostracization from that community. The only way to access any form of safety or protection is to fully commit mind, body, and soul to one set of rules and join with others who are willing to engage the same level of commitment to the same set of rules. At that level of commitment, there are always at least a few voices who know the rules, and you always have a flimsy claim to a Web 2.0 community.

In other words, so much about belonging in an online community is experienced as fear and disconnection. This is not a generalization, and there are people and communities that operate differently. But on the whole, many of the fragmented orbits online follow these mechanisms to the extent that we might be able to define "online culture" using these criteria. There is such a high degree of fragmentation that there really is no other way to define this diffuse multiverse. Online culture is the tendency to unfailingly commit to in-group norms to ensure continual belonging and protection from exclusion (in the best case) and ostracization and violence (in the worst case).

I can already hear the loud echoes of "but that's not all there is to online culture!" Of course not. The internet is everything everywhere all at once. It's nothing and nowhere. That's the trouble with defining it. I am working with the only possible definition that comes close to truthfully explaining its most consistent form and character. This form simultaneously engages the two fundamental elements of the human emotional spectrum: love and fear. The desire to love and be loved, i.e., the desire to belong to a community, is the same exact thing as the fear of exclusion and ostracization. They are the same emotion expressed as love versus fear.

The way the online world is currently structured leaves a lot more room for love than for fear. It's so easy to become our smallest selves with one less dimension, and it's even easier to see everyone else as something other than a human being, a two-dimensional mirage of a three-dimensional person. The ruling class in the attention economy encourages us to be very small—in terms of how we are represented in texts and avatars, and also in terms of how "petty" feelings are profitable. The smaller we are, the more we engage, the more we engage, the more addicted we become, the more addicted we are, and the more capital we generate. None of this feels very good, so we punish ourselves and each other even more. We need to break this cycle of attention and alienation.

In *We Will Not Cancel Us: And Other Dreams of Transformative Justice*, the abolitionist thought leader and activist adrienne maree brown presents us with a blueprint for breaking toxic cycles in social movement spaces. She writes: "In the longest term vision I can see, when we, made of the same miraculous material and temporary limitations as the systems we are born into, inevitably disagree, or cause harm, we will respond not with rejection, exile, or public shaming, but with clear naming of harm; education around intention impact and pattern breaking; satisfying apologies and consequences; new agreements and trustworthy boundaries; and lifelong healing resources for all involved."[33] While brown is writing about activist spaces both online and offline, achieving this kind of healing, accountability, and belonging is not possible within the mainstream internet and the attention economic system. For all the reasons outlined in this book, online culture is a punitive culture. It's a culture that thrives on rejection, exile, and public shaming. It's a culture that discourages pattern-breaking, apologizing, and learning.

Public online spaces owned by capitalist corporations cannot become the place where we find true community, belonging, and healing. These spaces are designed to thrive on our grief, disconnection, and illness. Yet the fact that we wake up every day and seek microdoses of collective effervescence is *hopeful*. We want to heal. We want change. We want community, belonging, and connection. This colonization of our attention and alienation of our being has not broken our fundamental humanity. We keep liking the likes and sharing the shares, hoping someone somewhere sees us and we see them, and for tiny moments we transcend. In those moments, it's the seeing that really means everything. Everything we do on the internet, we do to be seen. Ironically, outside of a staggering minority of people—viral YouTubers and TikTokers— we never actually *see* each other on the internet.

## LIBERATION

### Miracle

One day in 2022, I broke down crying in a classroom setting for the first time in many years of teaching at the college level. Everyone who knows me knows that I wear my heart on my sleeve, but that was unusual even for me. We were talking about the attention economy and how my young students are affected by our crippling dependence on digital media. To encourage an ongoing discussion about the positive aspects of digital and social media, I began to tell a story I had never told anyone before, or even thought about much until that day. When my parents were in the United States when I was a small child, I used to cry myself to sleep every night, hoping, praying, and dreaming of a technology that would enable me to see them through the phone. If I could just see them in real time, where they were, what they were doing, then it would not feel like they were so far away. It would be like they were right here with me. What a miraculous, magical technology that could be. (I was home with a cold that day, and this class happened over videoconferencing.)

Less than one percent of my time using internet services is devoted to video-calling friends and loved ones, except in the year 2020. Everything changed in 2020, but some changes were more permanent than others. When we thought the world was ending, we desperately grasped on to the ability to see our loved ones through the phone and the computer. I video-called my friends and family every day in March and most days in April, and fewer and fewer times after that. At the same time, video-conferencing became a normative element of many white-collar, middle-class jobs. My first year teaching as an assistant professor in 2020 was entirely online. Many people's jobs became permanently remote after this videoconferencing workplace revolution.

Even though I teach classes in person now, when I am sick, I will hold a class on videoconference. Before the pandemic, I imagine professors simply cancelled class and rested when they were sick. Videoconferencing for work has stuck around as an infallible legacy of the pandemic.

Videoconferencing for human connection gained a brief moment of popularity until we relaxed into the new postpandemic reality. Calling friends and family on video is a relatively common practice, as it was before the pandemic. From my perspective, it did not experience the same permanent surge from the pandemic as videoconferencing for work. Isn't that so bizarre? Part of the resistance to the attention economic system lies somewhere in reestablishing our ability to see each other—not as a username or an avatar but as a full human being with a face and a body.

## THE THIRD PATH

In her comprehensive manifesto *How To Do Nothing: Resisting the Attention Economy*, the Stanford professor Jenny Odell emphasizes that resistance cannot and should not mean unplugging from the attention economy. Unplugging is a privileged act; unplugging means we shut down completely from the difficulties we encounter every day and from the plights of the masses of people less fortunate than ourselves. At the same time, continuing to fall into the same cycles that monetize and abuse us cannot be the answer either. This calls for a third path to liberation from the attention economy: staying present, but reclaiming our attention within this space. Rather than ending up wherever the productive mazes wish to take us, we actively and intentionally decide where we go and what we do. Odell writes: "attention has its own margins . . . there is a significant portion of people for whom the project of day-to-day survival leads no attention for anything else; that's part of the viscous cycle too. That is why it's even more important for anyone who *does* have a margin— even the tiniest one—to put it to use in opening up margins further down the line. Tiny spaces can open up small spaces, small spaces can open up bigger spaces. If you can afford to pay a different kind of attention, you should."[34]

All the wisdom of the world is contained within this passage. Just as my job offline is to support students whose voices have been historically excluded, my job online is to listen to the stories of people whose voices have been historically excluded. The problem is that within the attention economy *there is no way to really know one another.* It is impossible to know anyone in their full and complete humanity, history, and identity in fleeting interactions in Web 2.0 space. Anything and everything we do in those spaces—even with the best of intentions of opening margins—profits Elon Musk, the comically bourgeoise "factory owner" of X, and Jeff Bezos, the villainous "landlord" of Amazon Web Services (AWS). They are always many steps ahead of us in figuring out new ways to profit from our every effort, even our effort to listen and engage with others fully.

We need to radically reimagine online spaces best suited to opening the margins. As engineers, programmers, and thought leaders envision Web 3.0, there is a disproportionate emphasis on design, ownership, and storage functions, and less focus on the diverse possibilities for new *social* characteristics. Web 3.0 emphasizes decentralized networks, but there is a disproportionate focus on building new economic structures in the likes of cryptocurrency and nonfungible tokens (NFTs).[35] The market has already been freed in popular dreams of Web 3.0, but society remains enslaved to mobile devices. The problem is that in neoliberal capitalism, the markets have remained free, so there is nothing revolutionary about the most popular imaginaries for Web 3.0.

There are, however, many extraordinary sociologists working to encapsulate visions for a revolutionary internet, in the radical social sense. There is currently space in the popular imagination—especially people outside of academia and in the tech sector, who design and implement web platforms—to more fully engage with the works and visions of sociologists such as Ruha Benjamin and Firuzeh Sookoh Valley.

One example is provided by Ruha Benjamin, who describes in *Viral Justice: How to Grow the World We Want* how Black TikTok users instigated a "cultural labor strike," withheld the work of content creation, and made the hashtag "BlackTiktokStrike" go viral on several key social media platforms.[36] Withholding the labor of being online is a surprisingly novel concept, perhaps because being online is not popularly considered work. Perhaps content creation is considered a gig, a side hustle, but I have made the case in this book that being online itself is a form of labor because it involves the use of labor-power measured as attention-time. Benjamin draws attention to the *power* behind such labor, as deconstrued by how marginalized communities of Black creators engaged in collective bargaining. Following their lead can result in all forms of collective bargaining outcomes, including bargaining for platforms and systems that do not buy and sell user attention. Nothing is off the table, really, because the entire attention economy relies on the engagement of users. When internet users recognize their power as labor and engage in collective solidarity with other workers/laborers, radical changes are possible, if not inevitable.

At a global level, Firuzeh Shokooh Valle outlines multiple radical reimaginations of how to use the internet in her book,

*In Defense of Solidarity and Pleasure: Feminist Technopolitics in the Global South.* Valle describes Indigenous participants at the Sulá Batsú technological co-op in Costa Rica as working to construct "a technology of feelings."[37] Such a construct is already a radical departure from existing ICT implementation in social media and the attention economy, where feelings are profitable units to be extracted, not celebrated. In this model, negative emotions thrive; however, in the technology of feelings imagined by the participants in her study, the emphasis is on positive emotions of solidarity and collective joy. More critically, there is an emphasis on "technology that feels," which at first glance may evoke generative AI and large language models. That is not what these activists have in mind, of course. The technology that feels here alludes to technology constructed with empathy and social support at the center rather than growth and profit. For example, "society and technology" is only one of several major areas of focus of the work done by members of Sulá Batsú. Equally central are projects that focus on constructing new economic structures that rely on solidarity rather than exclusion. The organization itself is built as a worker co-operative where all workers share any profits generated by projects and activities. The activists also centrally emphasize knowledge sharing, art, and culture, invoking technologies that holistically encapsulate the dimensionality of the human experience. Crucially, creating technology ultimately appears as a secondary goal of the co-op, building human relationships coming first. Valle often describes fascination with the way activists in the co-op develop bonds with the Indigenous women they work with, take extra care to amass expertise in Indigenous languages and cultural traditions so genuine human relationships based on shared meaning is constructed.

To transcend the attention economy, Web 3.0 needs to adhere to new standards across multiple dimensions that are different from the contemporary mainstream internet. Of course, these spaces *must* be collectively, publicly owned, but ownership is only the start. Many decentralized, encrypted peer-to-peer apps such as Signal and ProtonMail are already addressing the first problem.[38] Activist spaces increasingly rely on the privacy and freedom from surveillance afforded by these newer technologies to build resistance movements away from the itching wallets of the ruling class and threatening eyes of the states that protect their interest. However, as adrienne maree brown points out, activist spaces are not free from the pitfalls of the culture of exile and shaming even within their own communities. Engaging on the level of texts and avatars makes it really easy to treat people with rejection and punitive action. This is why we say the vilest things to each other textually that we would never say to people's faces. Without restoring the visibility of our humanity, we are always at the risk of treating each other in the subhuman ways promoted by the ruling class. Resistance cannot happen at the same level where we have been broken down. To truly resist, we need to level up.

My contribution to discussions around the construction of a radical new internet is this: Web 3.0 spaces must reinstate the ability to *see each other*. When we see each other and hear each other's voices, we reclaim our humanity on the internet, and that is the first step toward collectively defeating alienation 2.0. Video-conferencing technology can be at the center of such resistance. During the pandemic, I learned from becoming a professor that the virtual classroom has the same potential for transformation as the real classroom. A virtual classroom is the spiritual opposite of a comments section on social media. In the virtual classroom, we see each other, and one person speaks at a time while the rest of us listen; the possibility of opening up the margins here is limitless. In such spaces, we can get to know each other once again. We get to see and be seen, and we get to listen, learn, and grow. Here we renew the possibility to "respond not with rejection, exile, or public shaming, but with clear naming of harm; education around intention impact and pattern breaking; satisfying apologies and consequences; new agreements and trustworthy boundaries; and lifelong healing resources for all involved."[39]

Marx was convinced that the process of socially reproducing a socioeconomic system other than capitalism would be a necessarily violent process. This remains to be seen. What I *know* through multiple epistemologies including theory and data, as well as experience and intuition, is that reproducing an online economic system other than the attention economic system does not require violence—it requires the opposite: inner peace and healing. Reclaiming our attention is inseparable from healing our deepest selves so no algorithm is parasitic enough to dictate how we feel and act. Healing is a form of power that resides and remains in our bodies. Healing is directing our attention-time to whatever helps our individual and collective flourishing. Healing is refocusing. Healing is knowing that there is no such thing as individual flourishing without collective flourishing. When we heal, we may withhold our attention-labor. When we heal, we may demand radical alternatives to our online lives. When we heal, we may create something entirely new.

The internet of Web 3.0 and beyond has the potential to completely transform ourselves and our social relationships by integrating ideas of the passionate humanists, sociologists, and visionaries I have discussed here who occupy various marginalized intersections. My own humble contributions to these possibilities are ultimately a product of personal reflections as a teacher in a postpandemic world, who was at one point a small child with dreams that felt inseparable from magic. I live this dream every time I hold a class online, and when my family in Nepal gets to watch my toddler grow up through the phone.

Now I hope that the entire world can share this dream: that all of the internet may resemble an online classroom; a space where a desire to learn is the norm, and mistakes are as natural as breathing. A space where we see each other, hear each other, and respect each other, and nobody is making a profit from this process, so nobody gains anything or loses anything. A space where knowledge is shared, we learn together, we grow together. Perhaps there is hope yet for this dream too. All of my scientific research, theoretical abstractions, and personal experiences tell me that such a change in using the internet would be transformative. It would allow us to reclaim our attention. Rather than mindlessly and reactively engaging with each other at the lowest level 24/7, we would mindfully and intentionally engage with each other at the highest, most sincere levels for a set duration. In a way, this is not very different from Web 1.0 and the "opt-in" model—when I personally fell in love with the internet!

In this vision of Web 3.0 and beyond, the remainder of our leisure time—to the extent that we are privileged to have any—and our attention would be our own. We could step outside into the physical spaces we occupy, talk to our friends and neighbors, and walk in nature without worrying so much about the arbitrary approval of virtual strangers. There would be spaces for everyone to belong in the new internet, and we would all get a chance to take on speaking and listening roles in different spaces. Learning would be an ongoing process of our lives online and offline, without the fear of exile.

Eventually, we might even find perceptual level, *macrodoses* of collective effervescence.

# CONCLUSION

**W**hen I pitched this book to my editor a few years ago, I did not imagine that it would be a body of work that offered solutions. In the first week of my graduate studies at Stony Brook University, I was told repeatedly by multiple people that I was not admitted into the program to save the world. I'll admit that I was a tad disappointed. In my naïve undergraduate days, I assumed that the only purpose for studying the problems of society was so we could understand how to fix them. That turned out to be a ridiculous assumption in my graduate school's professional training, and here is a specific example of what I experienced.

Within my first few weeks at Stony Brook in 2014, I attended a Black Lives Matter protest led by Black graduate-student leaders in another department. The timing for this rally conflicted with a department brown-bag event in which a faculty member was giving a talk about their own research. I and a couple of my new friends from the program chose to go the rally instead of the research talk. The next time we went to our graduate seminar with the person who was department chair at the time, those of us who missed the talk were *berated*. Actually, everyone in class was berated because of the faux pas my friends and I made.

I can still feel the fear, shock, and horror of that day in my body when I revisit that moment. Having struggled with rules and authority my whole life, I suggested to this faculty member that we chose to attend the rally because Black folk were being murdered by the police regularly in the United States, so the protest seemed more important than a research talk. That was a mistake. If I wanted to save the world, I was told that I should quit school now and "become an activist." Academia is serious business. This is a real job that paid $17,000 a year in 2014. Serious grown-ups only.

If I hadn't been an international student on a visa, maybe I would have quit then, mostly because I was absolutely humiliated. But this graduate program was my ticket out of Nepali brahmin society, so I stayed in my lane from then on. I went to every research talk. I stopped going to protest marches and started writing peer-reviewed articles. Ultimately, my entire world began and ended with research and writing. In the early days of grad school, I wrote mostly about global food insecurity. I used statistics to understand what factors contributed to food security and insecurity in poor countries like my own. Why did I learn about one of the most pervasive and devastating forms of global inequality? So that I could get published in a high-impact journal and get an academic job! Sociology was not the study of society to fix the world. Turns out, sociology was the study of society to gain personal glory for all the main characters of reality.

I did the dance, my articles were published, I got a National Science Foundation Dissertation Award, and I landed a dream job at an elite liberal arts college. Once I understood the rules of the game, playing it became my entire identity. Failure was not an option for someone with a precarious immigration status. I did all the right things and was lucky in many places. I was fortunate to have excellent mentors, and they supported me every step of the way. There were people rooting for my failure too—people in power or authority who were toxic and abusive—but their disdain only pushed me harder to commit to my own well-being. For a time, I used healing in the Silicon Valley way: to get ahead in my own personal career.

But when I received my prized assistant professor title in 2020, *the world ended*. Everyone everywhere was forced—at least for a moment in time—to reconsider their priorities. There were many moments in March 2020 when I thought we had arrived at the end of the road for humanity, and that we were all going to die. In the face of something so total and final, all the things I had been taught to care about in graduate school suddenly seems so *silly*.

My dissertation defense was scheduled for a month into the pandemic, so it became the first defense in our department to be entirely online. Earning the doctorate was a huge deal at the end of my six years in this program. My defense was uneventful, except that my parents and Juni-*didi* and Shyam-*dai* and Suhel could join this virtual event. If the world hadn't ended, they would not have been at my defense. My mentors and all the people on the call were kind to me, and we all recognized the ultimate futility of this and every other professional activity. There were still people on the call who *grilled* me on the silliest of things as if any of it mattered. When I passed, Kevin popped a bottle of champagne in front of the Zoom call; then everyone signed off, and I took a nap.

When I woke up, I was Dr. Aarushi Bhandari, but the world was still ending. It was the darkest of times. The phones and the computers kept us "together." They kept the markets flowing and the classes going, and theses were defended. Without these devices, maybe we would have had a chance to rest and cope with the world ending. Instead, we carried our grief and our traumas in complete isolation and released these massive feelings into the network for contagion. Fear reigned. Outside of FaceTime calls with our loved ones, there was only fear. For much of that time I felt like I was reliving the traumas from Gyanendra's curfews. In place of neighborhood rooftop chatter, there was Twitter. Everyone was terrified, and everyone was shouting about it into an empty void. On the rooftops, we talked to one another and listened to one another. On Twitter we could only talk over one another and only listen to the loudest voice in the cacophony of fear. There was only fear: formless and omnipotent fear.

But in the FaceTime calls there was also love. *There was so much love.* When it feels like the world is ending, we suddenly see ourselves and our loved ones as perishable. When confronted with death, we understand the innate value of life. Even though we were so isolated, it was comforting to share these vulnerable experiences with our loved ones through the phone. Nothing seemed more important than the ability to see them and be with them and confront our shared being with all the knowledge of the fleeting nature of life. It was a beautiful experience unfolding amid the deadliest catastrophe.

By the time I began teaching Davidson students online in the fall of 2020, I cared most about supporting the well-being of my students. We had shared a kind of trauma most generations cannot conceive, and I refused to go back to pretending that my scholarship was isolated from my duties to humanity. My duty was to ensure that my students' education was symbiotic with their healing and the world's healing. If they engaged in activism, I would do nothing but encourage them. In this space, they would be rewarded for caring. From my years of teaching, it is abundantly clear that the students who devote themselves to social justice are usually students from marginalized communities: students of color, women and other marginalized genders, international students from the Global South, and students from LGBTQIA+ populations. The people who have been most harmed by our collective construction of reality are the most passionate about deconstructing and reconstructing our world.

In 2020–21, my online classes became a space where those passions were supported. In my virtual classrooms, I brought in speakers from marginalized races, genders, and castes from all around the world. I was extremely lucky that Davidson has a lot of resources, and they supported my efforts to compensate the speakers. Our speakers addressed topics ranging from capitalist fetishization of Asian women and sex tourism in the Philippines to the experiences of being excluded as a Dalit woman living in an Indian diaspora in the Netherlands. They spoke, and we listened and learned and asked questions. It was the best globalization class I ever taught. It was completely transformative.

Classes are back in person now, and there are many wonderful aspects of being in this physical place of learning. But in the two semesters when I taught fully online, I uncovered radical new possibilities for global spaces. The exciting news is that formal college settings don't have a monopoly over that kind of teaching and learning. At a time when monetization of artificial intelligence (AI) is mirroring the attention economy strategy of stealing the creative potential of human beings using poor machine imitations, teachers around the world are seeking pedagogical solutions. What AI can't do yet—if you are an AI engineer who has made it this far into my decidedly Marx-ish book, please don't get any ideas—is mimic full humans with faces and voices in ongoing live dialogue. (Dear reader, in the months since I wrote the previous sentence and now as I engage the copyediting process, AI *podcasts* have emerged—so I guess I was wrong about the imitating people with voices in ongoing live dialogue part. The dystopian reality I most fear now that AI technology is undergoing monetization is AI "therapists" on *Better Help* telling people things like "Wow, that sounds really difficult. You really deserve to treat yourself to that dragon egg replica that has been in your Amazon cart for the last four months.")

In my offline classrooms, I am transitioning to a more deliberative style of pedagogy, in which students sit and chat about ideas, books, and readings in real time. This "sit and chat" model could succeed online too if people are in small virtual spaces as their full, visible selves. That would still leave us with the problem of AI creating imitations of human art (and podcasts apparently) while humans suffer through mind-numbing socially unnecessary labor. But someone else more qualified will write *that* book soon enough.

In the process of writing *this* book, I realized how videoconference-based learning and social Web 3.0 spaces really could be the answer, at least in terms of changing the internet, if not the world. Although I feel strongly that transforming the former would have deeply transformative impacts on the latter. The thing is, "the world" is hard to change. That's probably why we have not done it yet, even though so many of us recognize that the way society is organized is far from ideal. The way we engage the internet, however, *is not that hard to change*. Compared to changing everything about society, changing the internet does not ask too much of us if we *really* think about it. We can stay in the place we are in already, use the same devices we already have, but we must learn to use them in a different way—in a way that supports our healing and connection rather than our illness and disconnection.

For workers in the factory system, overcoming alienation would require violent retaliation. This is not true for the work of being online in the attention economic system, which should be deeply encouraging. There are multiple examples of how an alternative to the attention economy can look, and I have provided my own musings, as well as examples, based on the work of several visionaries, including Ruha Benjamin and Jenny Oddell. Here I provide a final example of how a revolutionary alternative could look.

In 2010, the renowned sociologist Erik Olin Wright wrote *Envisioning Real Utopias*, in which he outlined multiple real world examples of structures and systems that feel utopian in the real world—for example, participatory democracy and worker co-ops.[1] One of his key examples of an *existing utopia* is *Wikipedia*. Looking back to Web 1.0 we see an example of an *online utopia*, but according to Wright this was an example of utopias in general. Wikipedia remains essentially unchanged, having resisted the attention economy and integration into the Web 2.0 model. Users still anonymously contribute knowledge to this massive information repository: they are not rewarded through social recognition, nor is their information bought and sold. Wikipedia continues to rely completely on donations and volunteer workers, and for the most part it provides a clear and relatively accurate overview on almost any topic imaginable—to the whole world, for free.[2] Wikipedia exists as a seemingly impossible public service that thrives even within the neoliberal attention economic system. Wikipedia shows that a very different way of using the internet can not only exist but thrive.

In this book I have demonstrated—starting with the global level and ending with the individual level—how information and communications technologies in their current form pose several threats to collective and individual flourishing. Yet I conclude that technology itself remains full of transformative possibilities. The technology remains *magical*.

What society needs to figure out is how to harness the magic for collective flourishing rather than harness collective trauma for capital. The process of change begins at the individual level by withholding attention-time and labor-power, and redirecting these really valuable resources consciously and intentionally toward constructive social goals: toward individual and collective healing. I have argued that everyone who is online is a worker in this sense, so everyone who is online has the power to create change. At the structural level, there are myriad examples of what change can and does look like, and I have added some of my own imaginations to the existing range of possibilities for the social structure of a transformative internet.

When it comes to transforming the internet, there is still hope. And unlike the cynical forgone conclusions about offline social reality envisioned by Karx Marx, this hope is innately peaceful. Peaceful and revolutionary. A contradiction, perhaps. A gift, no less.

Magic.

# NOTES

## INTRODUCTION

1. Ananda S. Verma and Gautam Navlakha, "People's War in Nepal: Genesis and Development," *Economic and Political Weekly* (2007): 1839–43.
2. Kunibert Raffer, *Unequal Exchange and the Evolution of the World System* (Springer, 1987).
3. Piet Strydom, *Discourse and Knowledge: The Making of Enlightenment Sociology*, vol. 1 (Liverpool University Press, 2000).
4. SeifDa'Na Khoury and Laura Khoury, "'Geopolitics of Knowledge': Constructing an Indigenous Sociology from the South," *International Review of Modern Sociology* (2013): 1–28.
5. Peta S. Cook, "'To Actually Be Sociological': Autoethnography as an Assessment and "Learning Tool," *Journal of Sociology* 50, no. 3 (2014): 269–82.
6. Karl Marx, *Marx: Selected Writings* (Hackett, 1994); and Christian Fuchs, *Digital Labour and Karl Marx* (Routledge, 2014).
7. The World Bank, World Development Indicators, 2020 (Washington, DC: The World Bank); International Telecommunication Union, ITU DataHub, https://datahub.itu.int/; Yearbook of International Organizations (Union of International Associations, 2000); GSMA, Mobile Gender Gap Data, https://www.gsmaintelligence.com/data/; and David Clark and Patrick Regan, "Mass Mobilization Protest Data, 2016," https://doi.org/10.7910/DVN/HTTWYL, Harvard Dataverse, V4.

8. Ruha Benjamin, *Viral Justice: How We Grow the World We Want* (Princeton University Press, 2022); and Jenny Odell, *How to Do Nothing: Resisting the Attention Economy* (Melville House, 2020).

9. Frank Moulaert, Bob Jessop, and Abid Mehmood, "Agency, Structure, Institutions, Discourse (ASID) in Urban and Regional Development," *International Journal of Urban Sciences* 20, no. 2 (2016): 167–87.

10. See Benjamin, *Viral Justice*; and Firuzeh Shokooh Valle, "Turning Fear Into Pleasure: Feminist Resistance Against Online Violence in the Global South," *Feminist Media Studies* 21, no. 4 (2021): 621–38.

## 1. THE INTERNATIONAL POLITICAL ECONOMY OF ATTENTION

1. Karl Marx, *Capital*. Vol. 1, *A Critique of Political Economy*, trans. Ben Fowkes (Penguin Classics, 1990); and Karl Marx, "Economic and Philosophic Manuscripts of 1844," in *Social Theory Re-Wired*, ed. Wesley Longhofer and Daniel Winchester (Routledge, 2016), 152–58.

2. Immanuel Wallerstein, *World-Systems Analysis: An introduction* (Duke University Press, 2020).

3. Christian Fuchs, *Digital Humanism: A Philosophy for 21st Century Digital Society* (Emerald Group, 2022); Christian Fuchs, "Information and Communication Technologies and Society: A Contribution to the Critique of the Political Economy of the Internet," *European Journal of Communication* 24, no. 1 (2009): 69–87; and Christian Fuchs, "Social Media, Alienation, and the Public Sphere," in *The Social Media Debate*, ed. Devan Rosen (Routledge, 2022), 53–76.

4. Jenny Odell, *How to Do Nothing: Resisting the Attention Economy* (Melville House, 2019).

5. Joseph E Stiglitz, "Knowledge as a Global Public Good," in *Global Public Goods: International Cooperation in the 21st Century*, ed. Inge Kaul, Isabella Grunberg, and Marc Stern (Oxford University Press, 1999), 308–25.

6. Sarah Babb and Alexander Kentikelenis, "Markets Everywhere: The Washington Consensus and the Sociology of Global Institutional Change," *Annual Review of Sociology* 47, no. 1 (2021): 521–41; and Ayse Kaya and Mike Reay, "How Did the Washington Consensus Move Within the IMF? Fragmented Change from the 1980s to the Aftermath of the 2008 Crisis," *Review of International Political Economy* 26, no. 3 (2019): 384–409.

7. Bradley W. Bateman, "There Are Many Alternatives: Margaret Thatcher in the History of Economic Thought," *Journal of the History of Economic Thought* 24, no. 3 (2002): 307–11.

8. Christian Fuchs, Wolfgang Hofkirchner, Matthias Schafranek, Celina Raffl, Marisol Sandoval, and Robert Bichler, "Theoretical Foundations of the Web: Cognition, Communication, and Co-operation. Towards an Understanding of Web 1.0, 2.0, 3.0," *Future Internet* 2, no. 1 (2010): 41–59.

9. G. Thomas Goodnight and Sandy Green, "Rhetoric, Risk, and Markets: The Dot-com Bubble," *Quarterly Journal of Speech* 96, no. 2 (2010): 115–40.

10. Jun Feng, Yu Chen, and Pu Liu, "Bridging the Missing Link of Cloud Data Storage Security in AWS," 7th IEEE Consumer Communications and Networking Conference (IEEE Xplore, 2010) 1–2; and Steven Gonzalez Monserrate, "The Cloud Is Material: On the Environmental Impacts of Computation and Data Storage" (MIT Schwarzman College of Computing, Winter 2022).

11. Michael H. Goldhaber, "The Attention Economy and the Net." *First Monday* 2, no. 4 (April 1997), https://doi.org/10.5210/fm.v2i4.519.

12. Karl Marx, *Das Capital*, vol. 1 (Penguin Classics, 1976), 284.

13. Sharlene Hesse-Biber, Patricia Leavy, Courtney E. Quinn, and Julia Zoino, "The Mass Marketing of Disordered Eating and Eating Disorders: The Social Psychology of Women, Thinness and Culture," *Women's Studies International Forum* 29, no. 2 (March 2006): 208–24.

14. Marx, *Das Capital*, vol. 1, 126.

15. Duncan K. Foley, "Recent Developments in the Labor Theory of Value," *Review of Radical Political Economics* 32, no. 1 (2000): 1–39; Gerald A. Cohen, "The Labor Theory of Value and the Concept of Exploitation," *Philosophy & Public Affairs* 8, no. 4 (1979): 338–60; and Donald F. Gordon, "What Was the Labor Theory of Value?," *American Economic Review* 49, no. 2 (1959): 462–72.

16. Marx, *Das Capital*, vol. 1, 284.

17. Marx, *Das Capital*, vol. 1, 129.

18. Leilasadat Mirghaderi, "Social Media Users' Free Labor in Iran: Influencers, Ethical Conduct and Labor Exploitation," *Frontiers in Sociology* 7 (2022): 1006146.

19. Marx, *Das Capital*, vol. 1, 270.

20. Pedro J. Rey, "Alienation, Exploitation, and Social Media," *American Behavioral Scientist* 56, no. 4 (2012): 399–420.

21. Marcello Musto, *Karl Marx's Writings on Alienation* (Palgrave Macmillan, 2021).

22. Marx, *Das Capital*, vol. 1, 375.

23. Karl Marx and Friedrich Engels, "The Communist Manifesto," in *Ideals and Ideologies: A Reader*, ed. Terence Ball, Richard Dagger, and Daniel I. O'Neill (Routledge, 2019), 243–55.

24. Mark Fisher, *Capitalist Realism: Is There No Alternative?* (John Hunt, 2022), 21–22.

25. Rahul De, Abhipsa Pal, Rupal Sethi, Sunil K. Reddy, and Chetan Chitre, "ICT4D Research: A Call for a Strong Critical Approach," *Information Technology for Development* 24, no. 1 (2018): 63–94.

26. Thomas E. Reifer, "Histories of the Present: Giovanni Arrighi & the Long Duree of Geohistorical Capitalism," *Journal of World-Systems Research* (2009): 249–56.

27. Christopher Chase-Dunn and Peter Grimes, "World-Systems Analysis," *Annual Review of Sociology* 21, no. 1 (1995): 387–417.

28. Giovanni Arrighi, *The Long Twentieth Century: Money, Power and the Origins of Our Times* (Verso, 1994).

29. Piya Mahtaney, *India, China and Globalization: The Emerging Superpowers and the Future of Economic Development* (Springer, 2007).

30. Kari Marie Norgaard, "The Sociological Imagination in a Time of Climate Change," *Global and Planetary Change* 163 (2018): 171–76.

31. Kenneth A. Gould, David N. Pellow, and Allan Schnaiberg, *Treadmill of Production: Injustice and Unsustainability in the Global Economy* (Routledge, 2015).

32. Mingyin Yao, "Examination of Underlying Factors in Success of TikTok," Proceedings of the 2021 International Conference on Enterprise Management and Economic Development (ICEMED, 2021), 296–301.

33. Congress.gov, "H.R.7521—118th Congress (2023–2024): Protecting Americans from Foreign Adversary Controlled Applications Act," March 14, 2024, https://www.congress.gov/bill/118th-congress/house-bill/7521.

34. Aimee Picchi, "TikTok Asks for Ban to Be Overturned, Calling It a 'Radical Departure' That Harms Free Speech," *CBS News*, June 20, 2024, https://www.cbsnews.com/news/tiktok-ban-lawsuit-bytedance-biden-congress/.

## 2. ICT4D, UNEQUAL EXCHANGE, AND NEOLIBERAL IMPERIALISM

1. David A. Smith, "Trade, Unequal Exchange, Global Commodity Chains: World-System Structure and Economic Development," in *Routledge Handbook of World-Systems Analysis*, ed. Salvatore Babones and Christopher Chase-Dunn (Routledge, 2012) 239–46.
2. Peyman Hekmatpour and Carrie M. Leslie, "Ecologically Unequal Exchange and Disparate Death Rates Attributable to Air Pollution: A Comparative Study of 169 Countries from 1991 to 2017," *Environmental Research* 212 (2022): 113161; and James Rice, "Ecological Unequal Exchange: International Trade and Uneven Utilization of Environmental Space in the World System," *Social Forces* 85, no. 3 (2007): 1369–92.
3. Firuzeh Shokooh Valle, *In Defense of Solidarity and Pleasure: Feminist Technopolitics from the Global South* (Stanford University Press, 2023).
4. Silvia Masiero, "Should We Still Be Doing ICT4D Research?," *Electronic Journal of Information Systems in Developing Countries* 88, no. 5 (2022): e12215.
5. Merlyna Lim, "The Politics and Perils of Dis/connection in the Global South," *Media, Culture & Society* 42, no. 4 (2020): 618–25.
6. GSMA, "Annual Report," 2022, https://media.gsma.com/assets/2022/annual_report.pdf.
7. Cher Ping Lim, Sungsup Ra, Brian Chin, and Tianchong Wang, "Information and Communication Technologies (ICT) for Access to Quality Education in the Global South: A Case Study of Sri Lanka," *Education and Information Technologies* 25, no. 4 (2020): 2447–62.
8. Aarushi Bhandari and Rebekah Burroway, "Hold the Phone! A Cross-National Analysis of Women's Education, Mobile Phones, and HIV Infections in Low-and Middle-Income Countries, 1990–2018," *Social Science & Medicine* 334 (2023): 116217.
9. David Speilman, Els Lecoutere, Simrin Makhija, and Bjorn Van Campenhout, "Information and Communications Technology (ICT) and Agricultural Extension in Developing Countries," *Annual Review of Resource Economics* 13, no. 1 (2021): 177–201.
10. Andrew K. Jorgenson, "Environment, Development, and Ecologically Unequal Exchange," *Sustainability* 8, no. 3 (2016): 227.

11. Vikram R. Bhargava and Manuel Velasquez, "Ethics of the Attention Economy: The Problem of Social Media Addiction," *Business Ethics Quarterly* 31, no. 3 (2021): 321–59.

12. Bhandari and Burroway, "Hold the Phone!"

13. Lim et al., "Information and Communication Technologies."

14. Aram Ziai, "The Discourse of 'Development' and Why the Concept Should Be Abandoned," *Development in Practice* 23, no. 1 (2013): 123–36.

15. Ronald Paul Hill and Bahram Adrangi, "Global Poverty and the United Nations," *Journal of Public Policy & Marketing* 18, no. 2 (1999): 135–46.

16. Yingqin Zheng, Mathias Hatakka, Sundeep Sahay, and Annika Andersson, "Conceptualizing Development in Information and Communication Technology for Development (ICT4D)," *Information Technology for Development* 24, no. 1 (2018): 1–14.

17. Millennium Summit, "United Nations Millennium Declaration," United Nations General Assembly Resolution 55/2, adopted September 8, 2000.

18. Maya Fehling, Brett D. Nelson, and Sridhar Venkatapuram, "Limitations of the Millennium Development Goals: A Literature Review," *Global Public Health* 8, no. 10 (2013): 1109–22.

19. Anuoluwapo Abosede Durofika and Edwin Chikata Ijeoma, "Neo-Colonialism and Millennium Development Goals (MDGs) in Africa: A Blend of an Old Wine in a New Bottle," *African Journal of Science, Technology, Innovation and Development* 10, no. 3 (2018): 355–66.

20. Severine Deneulin and Lila Shahani, eds., *An Introduction to the Human Development and Capability Approach: Freedom and Agency* (Earthscan, 2009).

21. Michael A. Clemens, Charles J. Kenny, and Todd J. Moss, "The Trouble with the MDGs: Confronting Expectations of Aid and Development Success," *World Development* 35, no. 5 (2007): 735–51.

22. Jeffrey D. Sachs, "From Millennium Development Goals to Sustainable Development Goals," *The Lancet* 379, no. 9832 (2012): 2206–11.

23. Fehling, Nelson, and Venkatapuram, "Limitations of the Millennium Development Goals: a Literature Review."

24. General Assembly, "Sustainable Development Goals," *SDGs Transform Our World* 2030, no. 10.1186 (2015).

25. General Assembly, "Resolution Adopted by the General Assembly on 19 September 2016." A/RES/71/1, October 3, 2016 (The New York Declaration), Tech. Rep (2015).

26. World Bank Group, *World Development Report 2016: Digital Dividends* (World Bank, 2016).

27. Nicole Eggers, Jessica Lynne Pearson, and Aurora Almada E. Santos, eds., *The United Nations and Decolonization* (Routledge, 2020).

28. Mark M. Mazower, *No Enchanted Palace: The End of Empire and the Ideological Origins of the United Nations* (Princeton University Press, 2009).

29. Mazower, *No Enchanted Palace*, 7.

30. Saul Dubow, "Smuts, the United Nations and the Rhetoric of Race and Rights," *Journal of Contemporary History* 43, no. 1 (2008): 45–74.

31. Mazower, *No Enchanted Palace*.

32. Nicolas Lemay-Hébert, "Exploring the Effective Authority of International Administrations from the League of Nations to the United Nations," *Journal of Intervention and Statebuilding* 11, no. 4 (2017): 468–89.

33. Susan Pedersen, *The Guardians: The League of Nations and the Crisis of Empire* (Oxford University Press, 2015).

34. Mazower, *No Enchanted Palace*, 21.

35. United Nations, "Security Council Fails to Recommend Full United Nations Membership for State of Palestine, Owing to Veto Cast by United States," April 18, 2024, https://press.un.org/en/2024/sc15670.doc.htm.

36. Eggers et al., *The United Nations and Decolonization*.

37. Lorna Llyod, "'A Most Auspicious Beginning': The 1946 United Nations General Assembly and the Question of the Treatment of Indians in South Africa," *Review of International Studies* 16, no. 2 (1990): 131–53.

38. Arundhati Roy, *The Doctor and the Saint: Caste, Race, and Annihilation of Caste, the Debate Between B.R. Ambedkar and M. K. Gandhi* (Haymarket, 2017).

39. Lloyd, "'A Most Auspicious Beginning,'" 131.

40. Ashwin Desai and Goolem Vahed, *The South African Gandhi: Stretcher-Bearer of Empire* (Stanford University Press, 2015).

41. John Boli and George M. Thomas, "World Culture in the World Polity: A Century of International Non-governmental Organization," *American Sociological Review* (1997): 171–90.
42. John W. Meyer, John Boli, George M. Thomas, and Francisco O. Ramirez, "World Society and the Nation-State," *American Journal of Sociology* 103, no. 1 (1997): 144–81.
43. Boli and Thomas, "World Culture in the World Polity," 171–90.
44. John Boli and George M. Thomas, *Constructing World Culture: International Nongovernmental Organizations Since 1875* (Stanford University Press, 1999).
45. Melanie M. Hughes, Lindsey Peterson, Jill Ann Harrison, and Pamela Paxton, "Power and Relation in the World Polity: The INGO Network Country Score, 1978–1998," *Social Forces* 87, no. 4 (2009): 1711–42.
46. Jason Beckfield, "Inequality in the World Polity: The Structure of International Organization," *American Sociological Review* 68, no. 3 (2003): 401–24.
47. Wesley Longhofer and Andrew Jorgenson, "Decoupling Reconsidered: Does World Society Integration Influence the Relationship Between the Environment and Economic Development?," *Social Science Research* 65 (2017): 17–29.
48. Rob Clark, "Technical and Institutional States: Loose Coupling in the Human Rights Sector of the World Polity," *Sociological Quarterly* 51, no. 1 (2010): 65–95.
49. Christopher Chase-Dunn, "Dependency and World-Systems Theories," *The Wiley Blackwell Encyclopedia of Race, Ethnicity and Nationalism* (Wiley Blackwell, 2015): 1–4.
50. Longhofer and Jorgenson, "Decoupling Reconsidered," 17–29.
51. Liam Swiss, "The Adoption of Women and Gender as Development Assistance Priorities: An Event History Analysis of World Polity Effects," *International Sociology* 27, no. 1 (2012): 96–119.
52. Aram Ziai, *Development Discourse and Global History: From Colonialism to the Sustainable Development Goals* (Taylor & Francis, 2016), 34.
53. Henry Bernstein, "Modernization Theory and the Sociological Study of Development," *Journal of Development Studies* 7, no. 2 (1971): 141–60.
54. Bernstein, "Modernization Theory," 141–60.
55. Ziai, *Development Discourse and Global History*, 30

56. The "Asian tigers"—Hong Kong, Singapore, South Korea, and Taiwan—underwent successful modernization. Notably, these are predominantly urban rather than agrarian nations, unlike much of the Global South.

57. Sarah S. Stroup and Wendy H. Wong, *The Authority Trap: Strategic Choices of International NGOs* (Cornell University Press, 2018).

## 3. CASTE SOCIETY AND DEVELOPMENT BAIT

1. For dependency, see Arno Tausch, "Globalisation and Development: The Relevance of Classical 'Dependency' Theory for the World Today," *International Social Science Journal* 61, no. 202 (2010): 467–88. For post-development, see Sally Matthews, "Post-Development Theory and the Question of Alternatives: A View from Africa," *Third World Quarterly* 25, no. 2 (2004): 373–84.

2. John J. Metz, "Development in Nepal: Investment in the Status Quo," *GeoJournal* 35 (1995): 175–84; and Christian Bjørnskov, "Do Elites Benefit from Democracy and Foreign Aid in Developing Countries?," *Journal of Development Economics* 92, no. 2 (2010): 115–24.

3. Nanda R. Shrestha, *In the Name of Development: A Reflection on Nepal* (University Press of America, 1997).

4. World Summit on the Information Systems, "Declaration of Principles: Building the Information Society: A Global Challenge in the New Millennium," 2005, https://www.itu.int/net/wsis/docs/geneva/official/dop.html.

5. Fraser Sugden, "Pre-Capitalist Reproduction on the Nepal Tarai: Semi-Feudal Agriculture in an Era of Globalisation," *Journal of Contemporary Asia* 43, no. 3 (2013): 519–45.

6. Nanda R. Shrestha, *In the Name of Development: A Reflection on Nepal* (University Press of America, 1997), 61.

7. Biswo Kalyan Parajuli, "Environmental Pollution and Awareness in Pokhara City: A Sociological Perspective," *Occasional Papers in Sociology and Anthropology* 6 (2000): 74-92.

8. World Bank, "World Development Indicators" (World Bank, 2024).

9. Aarushi Bhandari and Sam Shirazi, "Economic Dependency and Rural Exclusion: Explaining the Global Digital Divide, 1995 to 2014," *Sociology of Development* 8, no. 3 (2022): 239–71.

10. K. C. Dipendra, "Geographical Differences in the Evolutionary Pattern of Nepali Nongovernmental Organizations and Not for Profit Companies," National Institute of Development Administration, 2019, https://doi.org/10.14457/NIDA.the.2019.46.

11. Bhimrao Ramji Ambedkar, *Annihilation of Caste: The Annotated Critical Edition*, ed. S. Anand (Verso, 1936).

12. Neeta Rajbanshi and Lal B. Thapa, "Traditional Knowledge and Practices on Utilizing Medicinal Plants by Endangered Kisan Ethnic Group of Eastern Nepal," *Ethnobotany Research and Applications* 18 (2019): 1–9.

13. Adheesh A. Sathaye, *Crossing the Lines of Caste: Visvamitra and the Construction of Brahmin Power in Hindu Mythology* (Oxford University Press, 2015).

14. Bhimrao Ramji Ambedkar, *Castes in India: Their Mechanism, Genesis, and Development* (DigiCat, 2022).

15. Ambedkar, *Castes in India*.

16. Preeti Khattri et al., "Here & Now," *Nepali Times*, accessed August 14, 2024, https://www.nepalitimes.com/here-now/nepal-caste-attack-turns-deadly/.

17. Ambedkar, *Annihilation of Caste*, 2004, https://ccnmtl.columbia.edu/projects/mmt/ambedkar/web/readings/aoc_print_2004.pdf, 30.

18. Ambedkar, *Annihilation of Caste*, 32.

19. Jan E. M. Houben, "The Brahmin Intellectual: History, Ritual and 'Time Out of Time,'" *Journal of Indian Philosophy* 30, no. 5 (2002): 463–79.

20. Shrestha, *In the Name of Development*, 31.

21. Shrestha, *In the Name of Development*.

22. This occurred a few decades later when the "Washington consensus" adopting neoliberalism allowed them to continue expanding on this wealth by partnering with MNCs and making space for other foreign direct investment.

23. Melamchi Water Supply Project, accessed August 21, 2024, https://people.duke.edu/~charvey/Teaching/663_2014/Pancha/Melamchi_case.pdf.

24. Govinda R. Timilsina, Prakash Sapkota, and Jevgenijs Steinbuks, "How Much Has Nepal Lost in the Last Decade Due to Load Shedding? An Economic Assessment Using a CGE Model," World Bank Policy

Research Working Paper 8468, June 7, 2018; and Ratna Sansar Shrestha, "Electricity Crisis (Load Shedding) in Nepal, Its Manifestations and Ramifications," *Small* 8 (2010): 12–704.

25. Shrestha, *In the Name of Development*, 33.

26. Arturo Escobar, "Imagining a Post-Development Era? Critical Thought, Development and Social Movements," *Social Text* 31/32 (1992): 20–56.

27. Nancy Birdsall, David Ross, and Richard Sabot, "Inequality and Growth Reconsidered: Lessons from East Asia," *The World Bank Economic Review* 9, no. 3 (1995): 477–508.

28. Fernando Delbianco, Carlos Dabús, and María Ángeles Caraballo, "Income Inequality and Economic Growth: New Evidence from Latin America," *Cuadernos de Economía* 33, no. 63 (2014): 381–98.

29. Philip Nel, "Income Inequality, Economic Growth, and Political Instability in Sub-Saharan Africa," *Journal of Modern African Studies* 41, no. 4 (2003): 611–39.

30. Rita Jalali, "Financing Empowerment? How Foreign Aid to Southern NGOs and Social Movements Undermines Grass-Roots Mobilization," *Sociology Compass* 7, no. 1 (2013): 55–73.

31. Henry Veltmeyer, James Petras, and Steve Vieux, *Neoliberalism and Class Conflict in Latin America: A Comparative Perspective on the Political Economy of Structural Adjustment* (Springer, 2016).

32. Cristobal Kay. "For a Renewal of Development Studies: Latin American Theories and Neoliberalism in the Era of Structural Adjustment," *Third World Quarterly* 14, no. 4 (1993): 691–702.

33. David Reed, *Structural Adjustment and the Environment* (Routledge, 2019.)

34. "132 Dead by Rain Triggered Floods and Landslides in the Past 40 Days in Nepal," July 24, 2020, https://www.livemint.com/news/world/132-dead-by-rain-triggered-floods-and-landslides-in-past-40-days-in-nepal-11595583745410.html.

35. "Pollution Makes Life Hazardous in Kathmandu," accessed August 21, 2024, https://www.aninews.in/news/world/asia/pollution-makes-life-hazardous-in-kathmandu20220330201032/.

36. Amber N. French, "Dalits and Mental Health: Investigating Perceptions, Stigma and Barriers to Support in Kathmandu, Nepal," *Journal of Global Health Reports* 4 (2020): e2020009.

37. Kevin Matheson, "The Effects of Capitalism and Neoliberalism on Mental Health and Its Treatment: A Scoping Review and Sociohistorical Analysis of Developments in Clinical Psychology Following World War II" (University of Prince Edward Island, 2021).

## INTERLUDE 2. BEING EXTREMELY ONLINE AGAINST THE BACKDROP OF AN ARMED REVOLUTION

1. Madhav Joshi and Subodh Raj Pyakurel, "Individual-Level Data on the Victims of Nepal's Civil War, 1996–2006: A New Data Set," *International Interactions* 41, no. 3 (2015): 601–19.

2. Prakash Adhikari and Steven Samford, "The Nepali State and the Dynamics of the Maoist Insurgency," *Studies in Comparative International Development* 48 (2013): 457–81.

3. Rita Manchanda, "Maoist Insurgency in Nepal: Radicalizing Gendered Narratives," *Cultural Dynamics* 16, no. 2–3 (2004): 237–58.

4. Aditya Adhikari, *The Bullet and the Ballot Box: The Story of Nepal's Maoist Revolution* (Verso, 2014).

5. "Peacetime in a War Zone," *Nepali Times*, accessed August 21, 2024, https://archive.nepalitimes.com/news.php?id=14912#.Y5igRuzMLoo.

6. John Norris, "How Not to Wage a Counter-Insurgency: Nepal, the Maoists, and Human Rights," *Human Rights Brief* 11, no. 2 (2004): 4.

7. Amy Willesee and Mark Whittaker, *Love and Death in Kathmandu: A Strange Tale of Royal Murder* (Macmillan, 2004).

8. Michael Hutt, "The Royal Palace Massacre, Conspiracy Theories and Nepali Street Literature," in *Political Change and Public Culture in Post-1990 Nepal*, ed. Michael Hutt and Pratyoush Onta (Cambridge University Press, 2017), 39–55; and Barry Bearak, "A Witness to Massacre in Nepal Tells Gory Details," *New York Times*, June 8, 2001, https://www.nytimes.com/2001/06/08/world/a-witness-to-massacre-in-nepal-tells-gory-details.html.

9. "Profile: Paras Shah, Nepal's Errant Former Crown Prince," BBC News, December 14, 2010, https://www.bbc.com/news/world-south-asia-11992670.

10. Prashant Jha, *Battles of the New Republic: A Contemporary History of Nepal* (Oxford University Press, 2014).

11. Winnie Gobyn, "From War to Peace: The Nepalese Maoists's Strategic and Ideological Thinking," *Studies in Conflict & Terrorism* 32, no. 5 (2009): 420–38.

12. Kanak Mani Dixit, "Absolute Monarchy to Absolute Democracy," *Economic and Political Weekly* (2005): 1506–10.

13. Paul Routledge, "Nineteen Days in April: Urban Protest and Democracy in Nepal," *Urban Studies* 47, no. 6 (2010): 1279–99.

14. Randeep Ramesh et al., "Shoot-on-Sight Curfew Declared to Foil Nepal Rally," *The Guardian*, April 19, 2006, https://www.theguardian.com/world/2006/apr/20/nepal1.

15. "Nepal Extends Daytime Curfew," *New York Times*, April 20, 2006, https://www.nytimes.com/2006/04/20/world/asia/nepal-extends-daytime-curfew.html.

16. Peng Hwa Ang, Shyam Tekwani, and Guozhen Wang, "Shutting Down the Mobile Phone and the Downfall of Nepalese Society, Economy and Politics," *Pacific Affairs* 85, no. 3 (2012): 547–61.

17. Robin Jeffrey and Assa Doron, "The Mobile Phone in India and Nepal: Political Economy, Politics and Society," *Pacific Affairs* 85, no. 3 (2012): 469–81.

18. Mario Callegaro and Teresio Poggio, "Where Can I Call You? The 'Mobile (Phone) Revolution' and Its Impact on Survey Research and Coverage Error: A Discussion of the Italian Case," paper presented at the World Association of Public Opinion Research, Cadenabbia, Italy, June 24–26, 2004.

19. Ang, Tekwani, and Wang, "Shutting Down the Mobile Phone and the Downfall of Nepalese Society."

## 4. SOCIAL MOVEMENTS, COUNTER MOVEMENTS, AND DISCOURSE IN THE ATTENTION ECONOMY

1. For critical debates, see Zeynep Tufecki, *Twitter and Tear Gas: The Power and Fragility of Networked Protest* (Yale University Press, 2017). For support for ICT4D, see Laura Schelenz and Maria Pawelec, "Information and Communication Technologies for Development (ICT4D) Critique," *Information Technology for Development* 28, no. 1 (2022): 165–88; Calisto Kondowe and Wallace Chigona, "Rethinking Technology

Enabled Development: A Critique of the Neo-Liberal Perspective Embedded in ICT4D Studies," Proceedings of the 10th Conference of the International Development Informatics Association, August 23–24, 2018; William Mazzarella, "Beautiful Balloon: The Digital Divide and the Charisma of New Media in India," *American Ethnologist* 37, no. 4 (2010): 783–804; and Rahul De, Abhipsa Pal, Rupal Sethi, Sunil K. Reddy, and Chetan Chitre, "ICT4D Research: A Call for a Strong Critical Approach," *Information Technology for Development* 24, no. 1 (2018): 63–94.

2. Yousef Khalil, "Neoliberalism and the Failure of the Arab Spring," *New Politics* 15, no. 3 (2015): 77.

3. Thomas Häussler, "Civil Society, the Media and the Internet: Changing Roles and Challenging Authorities in Digital Political Communication Ecologies," *Information, Communication & Society* 24, no. 9 (2021): 1265–82.

4. Mehdi Mabrouk, "A Revolution for Dignity and Freedom: Preliminary Observations on the Social and Cultural Background to the Tunisian Revolution," in *North Africa's Arab Spring*, ed. George Joffe (Routledge, 2013), 121–31.

5. Lisa Anderson, "Demystifying the Arab Spring: Parsing the Differences Between Tunisia, Egypt, and Libya," *Foreign Affairs* 90, no. 3 (May/June 2011): 2–7.

6. James Glanz and John Markoff, "Egypt Leaders Found 'Off' Switch for Internet," *New York Times*, February 15, 2011.

7. Peng Hwa Ang, Shyam Tekwani, and Guozhen Wang, "Shutting Down the Mobile Phone and the Downfall of Nepalese Society, Economy and Politics," *Pacific Affairs* 85, no. 3 (2012): 547–61.

8. Jean Baudrillard, *Simulacra and Simulation*, trans. Sheila Faria Glaser (University of Michigan Press, 1994).

9. Mark Fisher, *Capitalist Realism: Is There No Alternative?* (Zero Books, 2009).

10. Andy Guess, Kevin Aslett, Joshua Tucker, Richard Bonneau, and Jonathan Nagler, "Cracking Open the News Feed: Exploring What U.S. Facebook Users See and Share with Large-Scale Platform Data," *Journal of Quantitative Description: Digital Media* 1 (2021).

11. Kara Alaimo, "How the Facebook Arabic Page 'We Are All Khaled Said' Helped Promote the Egyptian Revolution," *Social Media + Society* 1, no. 2 (2015): 2056305115604854.

12. Miriyam Aouragh and Anne Alexander, "The Arab Spring| the Egyptian Experience: Sense and Nonsense of the Internet Revolution," *International Journal of Communication* 5 (2011): 15.

13. Immanuel Wallerstein, *World-Systems Analysis* (Duke University Press, 2004), 46.

14. Christian Fuchs, "New Media, Web 2.0 and Surveillance," *Sociology Compass* 5, no. 2 (2011): 134–47.

15. Anita R. Gohdes, "Repression Technology: Internet Accessibility and State Violence," *American Journal of Political Science* 64, no. 3 (2020): 488–503.

16. Fuchs, "New Media."

17. Helga Tawil-Souri and Miriyam Aouragh, "Intifada 3.0? Cyber Colonialism and Palestinian Resistance," *Arab Studies Journal* 22, no. 1 (2014): 102–33.

18. Ori Schwarz, "Facebook Rules: Structures of Governance in Digital Capitalism and the Control of Generalized Social Capital," *Theory, Culture & Society* 36, no. 4 (2019): 117–41.

19. Gohdes, "Repression Technology," 491.

20. Edward Herman and Noam Chomsky, *Manufacturing Consent: The Political Economy of the Mass Media* (Vintage, 1998).

21. Johan Farkas and Christina Neumayer, "Disguised Propaganda from Digital to Social Media," *Second International Handbook of Internet Research*, ed. Jeremy Hunsinger, Matthew M. Allen, and Lisbeth Klasrup (Springer, 2020): 707–23.

22. Syeda Zainab Akbar, Ankur Sharma, Dibyendu Mishra, Ramaravind Kommiya Mothilal, Himani Negi, Sachita Nishal, Anmol Panda, and Joyojeet Pal, "Devotees on an Astroturf: Media, Politics, and Outrage in the Suicide of a Popular Film Star," in *Proceedings of the 5th ACM SIGCAS/SIGCHI Conference on Computing and Sustainable Societies*, 2022, 453–75.

23. Giovanni Arrighi, Terence K. Hopkins, and Immanuel Wallerstein, *Anti-Systemic Movements* (Verso, 2012).

24. Frantz Fanon, *The Wretched of the Earth*, trans. Richard Philcox (Grover, 2005), 62.

25. Bob Jessop, "Critical Semiotic Analysis and Cultural Political Economy," *Critical Discourse Studies* 1, no. 2 (2004): 159–74.

26. Frank Moulaert, Bob Jessop, and Abid Mehmood, "Agency, Structure, Institutions, Discourse (ASID) in Urban and Regional Development," *International Journal of Urban Sciences* 20, no. 2 (2016): 167–87.

27. Mohan J. Dutta and Ngā Hau, "Voice Infrastructures and Alternative Imaginaries: Indigenous Social Movements Against Neocolonial Extraction," in *The Rhetoric of Social Movements*, ed. Nathan Crick (Routledge, 2020), 254–68.

28. Nick Estes, *Our History Is the Future: Standing Rock Versus the Dakota Access Pipeline, and the Long Tradition of Indigenous Resistance* (Haymarket, 2024).

29. Tony D. Sampson, *Virality: Contagion Theory in the Age of Networks* (University of Minnesota Press, 2012).

30. Arrighi, Hopkins, and Wallerstein, *Anti-Systemic Movements*.

31. Edward S. Herman and Noam Chomsky, "Manufacturing Consent," in *Power and Inequality* (Routledge, 2021), 198–206.

32. Jason C. Mueller and Steven Schmidt, "Revisiting Culture and Meaning-Making in World-Systems Analysis: A Proposal for Engaging with the Cultural Political Economy Approach," *Critical Sociology* 46, no. 4–5 (2020): 711–28.

33. Fisher, *Capitalist Realism: Is There No Alternative?*

34. Aarushi Bhandari and Sam Shirazi, "Economic Dependency and Rural Exclusion: Explaining the Global Digital Divide, 1995 to 2014," *Sociology of Development* 8, no. 3 (2022): 239–71.

35. Finn Brunton, *Digital Cash: The Unknown History of the Anarchists, Utopians, and Technologists Who Created Cryptocurrency* (Princeton University Press, 2020).

36. Asef Bayat, *Revolution Without Revolutionaries: Making Sense of the Arab Spring* (Stanford University Press, 2020).

37. Francesca Sobande, "Woke-Washing: 'Intersectional' Femvertising and Branding 'Woke' Bravery," *European Journal of Marketing* 54, no. 11 (2019): 2723–45.

38. Yu-Hao Lee and Gary Hsieh, "Does Slacktivism Hurt Activism? The Effects of Moral Balancing and Consistency in Online Activism," in *Proceedings of the SIGCHI Conference on Human Factors in Computing Systems*, 2013, 811–20.

39. Marcia Mundt, Karen Ross, and Charla M. Burnett, "Scaling Social Movements Through Social Media: The Case of Black Lives Matter," *Social Media+ Society* 4, no. 4 (2018): 2056305118807911.

40. Cagri Toraman, Furkan Şahinuç, and Eyup Halit Yilmaz, "Blacklivesmatter 2020: An Analysis of Deleted and Suspended Users in Twitter," In *Proceedings of the 14th ACM Web Science Conference*, 2022, 290–95.

# 5. MICRODOSING COLLECTIVE EFFERVESCENCE

1. Bertell Ollman, *Alienation: Marx's Conception of Man in a Capitalist Society*, 2nd ed. (Cambridge University Press, 1977).

2. Karl Marx, *Capital*. Vol. 1, *A Critique of Political Economy*, trans. Ben Fowkes (Penguin Classics, 1990).

3. Bhimrao Ramji Ambedkar, "Castes in India: Their Mechanism, Genesis and Development," *Readings in Indian Government and Politics, Class, Caste, Gender* (2004), 138.

4. Karl Marx, "Economic and Philosophic Manuscripts of 1844," in *Social Theory Re-Wired*, ed. Wesley Longhofer and Daniel Winchester (Routledge, 2016), 152–58.

5. Karl Marx and Friedrich Engels, "The Communist Manifesto," in *Ideals and Ideologies: A Reader*, ed. Terence Ball, Richard Dagger, and Daniel I. O'Neill (Routledge, 2019), 243–55.

6. Amy Wendling, *Karl Marx on Technology and Alienation* (Springer, 2009), 169.

7. Pedro J. Rey, "Alienation, Exploitation, and Social Media," *American Behavioral Scientist* 56, no. 4 (2012): 399–420.

8. Ying Ge, Jun Se, and Jingfu Zhang, "Research on Relationship Among Internet-Addiction, Personality Traits and Mental Health of Urban Left-Behind Children," *Global Journal of Health Science* 7, no. 4 (2015): 60; and Louis Leung, "Predicting Internet Risks: A Longitudinal Panel Study of Gratifications-Sought, Internet Addiction Symptoms, and Social Media Use Among Children and Adolescents," *Health Psychology and Behavioral Medicine: An Open Access Journal* 2, no. 1 (2014): 424–39.

9. Yonghui Feng, Yutong Ma, and Qisong Zhong, "The Relationship Between Adolescents' Stress and Internet Addiction: A Mediated-Moderation Model," *Frontiers in Psychology* 10 (2019): 2248.

10. William R. Marchand, "Mindfulness-based Stress Reduction, Mindfulness-based Cognitive Therapy, and Zen Meditation for Depression, Anxiety, Pain, and Psychological Distress," *Journal of Psychiatric Practice* 18, no. 4 (2012): 233–52.

11. Paul Verhaeghen, "Mindfulness as Attention Training: Meta-Analyses on the Links Between Attention Performance and Mindfulness

Interventions, Long-Term Meditation Practice, and Trait Mindfulness," *Mindfulness* 12 (2021): 564–81.

12. Joanna Macy, *Mutual Causality in Buddhism and General Systems Theory: The Dharma of Natural Systems* (Suny Press, 1991).

13. Jon Kabat-Zinn, "Mindfulness-based Stress Reduction (MBSR)," *Constructivism in the Human Sciences* 8, no. 2 (2003): 73.

14. Wendy Kersemaekers, Silke Rupprecht, Marc Wittmann, Chris Tamdjidi, Pia Falke, Rogier Donders, Anne Speckens, and Niko Kohls, "A Workplace Mindfulness Intervention May Be Associated with Improved Psychological Well-Being and Productivity. A Preliminary Field Study in a Company Setting," *Frontiers in Psychology* 9 (2018): 195.

15. Jaime Kucinskas,. *The Mindful Elite: Mobilizing from the Inside Out* (Oxford University Press, 2018).

16. Kevin Healy. "Disrupting Wisdom 2.0: The Quest for 'Mindfulness' in Silicon Valley and Beyond," *Journal of Religion, Media and Digital Culture* 4, no. 1 (2015): 67–95.

17. Bhimrao Ramji Ambedkar, *The Buddha and His Dhamma: A Critical Edition* (Oxford University Press, 2011); and Nicolas Jaoul, "Citizenship in Religious Clothing?: Navayana Buddhism and Dalit Emancipation in Late 1990s Uttar Prradesh," *Focaal* 2016, no. 76 (2016): 46–68.

18. bell hooks, *Teaching to Transgress: Education as the Practice of Freedom* (Routledge, 2014).

19. bell hooks, "Theory as Liberatory Practice," *Yale Journal of Law & Feminism* 4 (1991): 1.

20. Tony Sampson, *Virality: Contagion Theory in the Age of Networks* (University of Minnesota Press, 2012).

21. Karel Lehmert, Eva Ambrozova, Vratislav Pokorny, and Jiri Kolenak, "Microdosing of Psychoactive Substances in Business Practice," *Businesses* 1, no. 3 (2021): 196–204.

22. Ben Sessa, *The Psychedelic Renaissance: Reassessing the Role of Psychedelic Drugs in 21st Century Psychiatry and Society* (Aeon, 2020).

23. Michael Pollan, *How to Change Your Mind: What the New Science of Psychedelics Teaches Us About Consciousness, Dying, Addiction, Depression, and Transcendence* (Penguin, 2018).

24. Ben Sessa, "MDMA and PTSD Treatment: 'PTSD: From Novel Pathophysiology to Innovative Therapeutics'," *Neuroscience Letters* 649 (2017): 176–80; and Michael Winkelman, "Psychedelics as Medicines

for Substance Abuse Rehabilitation: Revaluating Treatments with LSD, Peyote, Ibogaine and Ayahuasca," *Current Drug Abuse Reviews* 7, no. 2 (2014): 101–16.

25. Lynne Segal, *Radical Happiness: Moments of Collective Joy* (Verso, 2017).

26. Émile Durkheim, "The Elementary Forms of Religious Life," in *Social Theory Re-wired* (Routledge, 2016).

27. Bernard Rimé and Dario Páez, "Why We Gather: A New Look, Empirically Documented, at Émile Durkheim's Theory of Collective Assemblies and Collective Effervescence," *Perspectives on Psychological Science* 18, no. 6 (2023): 1306–30.

28. Aarushi Bhandari, "Taylor Swift's Eras Tour Is a Potent Reminder That the Internet Is Not Real Life," The Conversation, August 4, 2023, https://theconversation.com/taylor-swifts-eras-tour-is-a-potent -reminder-that-the-internet-is-not-real-life-209325.

29. Anindya Das, "Pharmaceutical Industry and the Market: The Case of Prozac and Other Antidepressants," *Asian Journal of Psychiatry* 4, no. 1 (2011): 14–18.

30. Pietje M. Verbeek-Heida and Edith F. Mathot, "Better Safe Than Sorry—Why Patients Prefer to Stop Using Selective Serotonin Reuptake Inhibitor (SSRI) Antidepressants But Are Afraid to Do So: Results of a Qualitative Study," *Chronic Illness* 2, no. 2 (2006): 133–42.

31. Mark Fisher, *Capitalist Realism: Is There No Alternative?* (John Hunt, 2022).

32. Gayatri Chakravorty Spivak, "Can the Subaltern Speak?," in *Imperialism* (Routledge, 2023), 171–219.

33. adrienne maree brown, *We Will Not Cancel Us: And Other Dreams of Transformative Justice* (AK Press, 2020), 11.

34. Jenny Odell, *How to Do Nothing: Resisting the Attention Economy* (Melville House, 2019), 94.

35. Richard E Ferdig, Michael Cohen, Eric Ling, and Richard Hartshorne, "Examining Blockchain Protocols, Cryptocurrency, NFTs, and Other Web 3.0 Affordances in Teacher Education," *Journal of Technology and Teacher Education* 30, no. 1 (2022): 5–19.

36. Ruha Benjamin, *Viral Justice: How to Grow the World We Want* (Princeton University Press, 2022).

37. Firuzeh Shokooh Valle, *In Defense of Solidarity and Pleasure: Feminist Technopolitics from the Global South* (Stanford University Press, 2023), 63.

38. Anthony Mills and Katharine Sarikakis, "Reluctant Activists? The Impact of Legislative and Structural Attempts of Surveillance on Investigative Journalism," *Big Data & Society* 3, no. 2 (2016): 2053951716669381.

39. brown, *We Will Not Cancel Us*, 11.

## CONCLUSION

1. Erik Olin Wright, *Envisioning Real Utopias* (Verso, 2020).

2. Ping Wang and Xiaodan Li, "Assessing the Quality of Information on Wikipedia: A Deep-Learning Approach," *Journal of the Association for Information Science and Technology* 71, no. 1 (2020): 16–28.

# INDEX

Adhikara, Aditya, 98
algorithms, 6, 29, 41, 128–29, 139–40;
  and attention economy, 33–34;
  manipulating users, 11, 23–25, 40;
  mining user information, 16–20;
  and virality, 26–27, 131
alienation, 5, 7, 29, 173; and the
  attention economy, 32–36, 149,
  151, 152, 162, 168, 170; Marxist
  definition, 6, 30–32, 149–51;
  resistance to, 172, 179, 187; and
  unequal exchange, 10, 11, 13–14
alternative imaginaries, 11, 128,
  130–31, 136, 140–42. *See also*
  imaginaries
Amazon Web Services, 16, 176
Ambedkar, Bhimrao Ramji, 85,
  87–88, 148, 160
anarchist movements, 129, 140–41
*Annihilation of Caste*, 87
apartheid, 56, 58, 60
Apple Inc., 17, 40, 128, 139, 166
Arab Spring, 114–15, 117, 142
artificial intelligence (AI), 186–87

ASID model, 11, 127–28, 139
attention, 9, 10, 13–14, 29, 164, 172,
  173; as a commodity, 22–23,
  25–29, 34, 40, 49–50; and
  meditation, 156–57; as resistance,
  162, 175–76, 180
attention capitalism, 28, 35
attention economy, 7, 10, 12, 94,
  118, 138, 140, 162, 180; and
  algorithms, 11; as capital, 149–50,
  170; and children, 153–54; and
  development, 37–39, 46–47, 70;
  definition of, 5–6, 14–18, 32–36,
  40; labor in, 24–29, 49, 126, 152–
  53, 163, 177, 180; Odell, Jenny, 9,
  14; resistance to, 175; surveillance
  in, 118–20, 121–22, 129, 179; and
  social movements, 123–26
attention marketplace, 20, 23,
  41–42
attention-time, 20, 26, 28–29, 32–36,
  126, 180, 189
*The Authority Trap: Strategic Choices
  of International NGOs*, 71

Baudrillard, Jean, 116
Bayat, Aset, 142
Benjamin, Ruha, 9, 12, 177, 188
Bezos, Jeff, 176
Bhattrai, Baburam, 98–99, 104
Biden, Joe, 41
Black Lives Matter, 142–43, 182–83
brown, adrienne maree, 172–73, 179
Buddhism, 155–58, 160
*The Bullet and the Ballot Box*, 98
Burroway, Rebekah, 50–51
ByteDance Ltd. 41, 128

*Das Capital*, 13, 17–19, 31–32, 148, 151
capital, 14, 149–50
capitalism, 27–28, 30, 94, 147–48;
    late capitalism, 151–52; Marxist
    definition of, 18–19; and
    neoliberalism, 15, 46, 51, 65, 70,
    75, 92–94; and world-systems
    theory, 37–38
*Capitalist Realism: Is There No
    Alternative?* 33, 116–17, 136–37, 143
caste, 10, 45, 59–61, 74, 76, 145;
    Brahmin, 1, 3, 4, 148–49, 160;
    definition of, 84–86. *See also*
    Hinduism, India, Nepal
*Castes in India: Their Mechanism,
    Genesis, and Development*, 85, 148
child marriage, 4, 85, 145–46, 148
China, 38, 41, 128
Chomsky, Noam, 120
climate change. *See* environment
collective effervescence, 107, 167–68,
    173, 181
colonization, 66–68, 72

commodities, 19, 21–22
commodity fetishism, 31
*The Communist Manifesto*, 32, 151
conspiracy theories, 169, 170
Covid-19 pandemic, 68–69, 158–59,
    169, 175, 179–80, 184–86
cryptocurrency, 141, 176
cultural political economy (CPE),
    126–27, 134–37
cyberoptimism, 4, 36
cyberutopianism, 4, 163

Dakota Access Pipeline, 130–31
*The Dalit Buddhist Movement*, 160
dependency theory, 73, 91
depressive hedonia, 33–34
development, 5, 7, 10, 51, 71; agendas,
    52–54, 57, 72; agents, 37, 45, 47,
    83–84, 62; and caste, 87–92;
    critiques of, 73, 91; foreign aid,
    91–92; modernization, 66–70, 77,
    80; world polity, 62–66. *See also*
    ICT4D
*Development Discourse and Global
    History: From Colonialism to the
    Sustainable Development Goals*, 66
digital inequality, 79–83, 138
discourse, 11, 123, 126, 129–31, 138–40,
    171
distraction, 24, 29, 34
Du Bois, W. E. B. 56
Durkheim, Émile, 167

Economic and Philosophic
    Manuscripts of 1844 (Marx),
    13, 31

economy of attention. *See* attention
economy
education, 48–51, 88, 97–98, 104,
185–86
entertainment, 24–25, 28–29
environment, 38–39, 46, 54, 64–66,
70, 130; air pollution, 93–94
*Envisioning Real Utopias*, 188

Facebook, 17, 19, 116–17, 119
Fanon, Frantz, 121
Fisher, Mark, 33, 116–17, 136–37, 143
Fuchs, Christian, 8, 14

Gandhi, Mohandas Karamchand,
59–60
gender, 1, 4, 134, 148–49, 162, 185–86
Ghodes, Anita, 119–20
Global North, 47, 70, 93–94
Global South, 10, 37, 133; elites, 89,
91; and environmentalism, 65;
ICT4D 41–42, 46–52, 70, 74–76,
79–81, and neoliberalism, 67–69,
72, 92–94. *See also* development
Google LLC 49, 138, 166
GSM Association (GSMA), 9, 10,
47–49
Gyanendra Bir Bikram Shah, 3,
102–12, 116, 117

hashtags, 130–31, 143, 169
healing, 12, 36, 162, 164, 180, 189
health, 48–50
Herman, Edward, 120
Hinduism, 84–87, 120, 146, 148, 160.
*See also* caste, India, Nepal

hooks, bell, 161–62
horizontal communication, 114–15
*How to Do Nothing: Resisting the
Attention Economy*, 9, 14, 175
hyperreality, 116–17

ICT4D (ICT for development),
10, 37, 42, 52, 79–82, 113; and
the attention economy, 70–72,
74–75; unequal exchange, 46–50;
United Nations millennium
development goals, 53–54, 61–62.
*See also* development
imaginaries, 127, 135–43. *See also*
alternative imaginaries
imperialism, 67, 71–72
*In Defense of Solidarity and Pleasure:
Feminist Technopolitics in the
Global South*, 47, 61, 178
*In the Name of Development: A
Reflection on Nepal*, 73
India, 38, 58–59, 120, 155–56
Indigenous peoples, 130, 178.
*See also* alternative imaginaries,
Nepal
influencers. *See* social media
information and communication
technologies (ICTs), 1, 5, 15, 24,
74; access, 41, 47, 50–51, 54, 75–76,
79–81; authoritarian shutdown
of, 3, 103–12, 115–17; international
political economy of, 9; and
social movements, 113, 143.
*See also* ICT4D
intellectual class, 87–92. *See also*
caste, Nepal

international development.
    *See* development
IMF (International Monetary
    Fund), 93
international non-governmental
    organizations (INGOs), 51–52,
    71, 79, 82–84
international political economy of
    attention. *See* attention economy
internet, 3–4, 8, 47; addiction, 153–54,
    164, 172; authoritarian shutdown
    of, 3, 103–12; online communities,
    3–4, 170–71; online culture,
    171–73; and social movements,
    121–26, 133–34, 137–38; Web, 1.0
    5, 8, 16, 24, 37; Web, 2.0 5, 6, 8,
    11, 17–19, 24, 28–29, 37, 116, 163;
    Web, 3.0 6, 12, 36, 176, 178–81;
    World Wide Web, 12, 15, 36–37.
    *See also* ICT4D, information and
    communication technologies
iPhone, 17, 42, 122. *See also*
    smartphones

Jessop, Bob, 135
*Journal of World Systems Research*, 137

*Karl Marx on Technology and
    Alienation*, 151
Kathmandu, 1, 3, 43–45, 51–52, 95–112.
    *See also* Nepal
Kucinskas, Jamie, 157–58

labor, 14, 17, 21, 27–28
labor-power, 27–29, 148
labor theory of value, 20–22, 25–26,
    29, 148
Lie, Trygve, 57–58

*Manufacturing Consent*, 120
Marx, Karl, 8, 13, 17–19, 20–21, 24,
    150, 180, 189. *See also* commodity
    fetishism, labor-power, labor
    theory of value, species being,
    surplus value, use value
Marxism, 5, 6, 9, 13–14, 37, 132
Mass Mobilizations Data Project, 9,
    11, 120–22
Mazower, Mark, 55–56
meditation, 156–58, 166
mental health, 7, 94, 165–66
Meta Platforms Inc. 40, 49, 119,
    128, 139
methods, 7–9
microdosing, 165–68
Microsoft, 41
*The Mindful Elite: Mobilizing from
    the Inside Out*, 157
mindfulness. *See* meditation
mobile phones. *See* smartphones
modernization. *See* development
Modi, Narendra, 120
Mubarak, Hosni, 115, 117
multinational corporations
    (MNCs), 39–40, 42, 69–70
Musk, Elon, 176

Nehru, Jawaharlal, 58–60
neoliberalism, 10, 39, 46, 136–37,
    142–43; definition of, 15; and
    development, 51–52, 69–72, 75,
    79–81, 92–94
Nepal, 38, 43–45, 51–52, 73–74; caste,
    84–88, 91, 100–101, 145–47; Civil
    War, 3, 10, 78, 86, 95–112, 116;
    Indigenous populations, 76–78,
    85–86; infrastructure, 89–90;

monarchy, 99–112; Operation Romeo, 99–101; stereotypes, 155–56

*No Enchanted Palace: The End of Empire and the Ideological Origins of the United Nations*, 55

nonfungible tokens (NFTs), 176

objectivity, 7, 98, 171

Odell, Jenny, 9, 14, 36, 175–76, 188

online attention economy. *See* attention economy

online culture. *See* internet

online proletariat, 14, 18, 24–29, 34. *See also* attention economy

Pandit, Vijaya Laxmi, 60

platforms, 19, 119, 128–29, 177. *See also* internet, social media

political economy, 7, 37–42. *See also* attention economy, world systems theory

positionality, 88, 97–98, 104

postdevelopment theory, 73, 91

Prachanda (Pushpa Kamal Dahal), 98–99, 104

praxis, 12, 88, 162, 164

propaganda, 120–21, 133, 139; in Nepal Civil War, 100, 103–4, 110–11

Protecting Americans from Foreign Adversary Controlled Applications Act, 41

ProtonMail, 179

*Radical Happiness: Moments of Collective Joy*, 167

rage bait, 25

Reddit, 24, 138, 169

refolutions, 142

*Revolution Without Revolutionaries: Making Sense of the Arab Spring*, 142

rural development. *See* development

rural populations, 75–76, 80–83

Sachs, Jeffery, 53

Segal, Lynne, 167–68

selfhood, 5–6, 14, 17, 34, 50

Shirazi, Sam, 79

Shrestha, Nanda, 73–74, 76–77, 88, 90, 91–92

Signal, 169, 179

slacktivism, 11, 143, 168, 169

smartphones, 19, 40, 47–48, 50–51, 122

Smuts, Jan, 56–58, 60

Snapchat, 19–20

social media, 16–20, 23, 24, 41, 116–17; and development, 47–50; influencers, 26; as labor, 32–33; and propaganda, 120; and social movements, 117, 128–29, 137–43, 169; and surveillance, 118–19

social movements, 5, 7, 14, 128–29, 131–32, 136; counter movements, 11, 14, 142–43; and ICTs, 113, 137–39; offline protest participation, 140–41; online, 11, 143, 169–70; violent protests, 123–26. *See also* state violence

South Africa, 58–61

species being, 29, 31, 34, 150

Sri Lanka, 51

state violence, 118, 120–26, 129–30, 142; in Nepal, 99–101, 106

Stroup, Sarah, 71

structural adjustment, 65, 92–93

Sulá Batsú, 178

surplus value, 21–23, 27, 148

*Teaching to Transgress*, 161

technological ruling class, 5, 11, 14, 18, 35, 40, 49

Thatcher, Margaret, 15

TikTok, 16, 19, 24, 26–27, 41, 173

treadmill of production, 39

Twitter. *See* X

unequal exchange, 46–47, 50, 74–75

United Nations, 10, 47, 51–52; history of, 55–59; millennium development goals (MDGs), 53–54; sustainable development goals (SDGs), 52, 54

United States, 38, 40, 128, 130, 139–40

unplugging, 175

U.S. Telecommunications Act of, 1996–15, 36

use value, 6, 19–23, 25–28

Valle, Firuzeh Sookoh, 12, 47, 61, 177–78

videoconferencing, 7, 12, 174–75, 179

*Viral Justice: How to Grow the World We Want*, 9, 177

virality, 11, 26–27, 131, 136, 163, 167

*Virality: Contagion Theory in the Age of Networks*, 163

Wallerstein, Immanuel, 118

*We Will Not Cancel Us: And Other Dreams of Transformative Justice*, 172

Wendling, Amy, 151

Western imperialism, 45, 46–47

Wikipedia, 12, 188

Wong, Wendy, 71

world attention economic system, 37, 39, 74; definition of, 37, 40. *See also* attention economy

World Bank, 93, 127

world culture, 63, 71

World Data Bank, 9

world polity, 62–66

world society, 63

World Summit on the Information Systems (WSIS), 75

world systems theory, 9, 13, 69–70, 79, 118, 121, 134; and development, 73, 91; overview of, 37–39; and social movements, 131–32; and unequal exchange, 46

World Wide Web. *See* internet

*Wretched of the Earth*, 121

Wright, Erik Olin, 12, 188

X 17, 19, 24, 29, 116, 120, 138, 169, 176

YouTube, 173

Ziai, Aram, 66, 68

GPSR Authorized Representative: Easy Access System Europe, Mustamäe tee
50, 10621 Tallinn, Estonia, gpsr.requests@easproject.com

www.ingramcontent.com/pod-product-compliance
Lightning Source LLC
Chambersburg PA
CBHW032133020426
42334CB00016B/1151